GLOBAL VALUES 101

A Short Course

EDITED BY

Kate Holbrook
Ann S. Kim
Brian Palmer
Anna Portnoy

BEACON PRESS
Boston

BEACON PRESS
25 Beacon Street
Boston, Massachusetts 02108-2892
www.beacon.org

Beacon Press books
are published under the auspices of
the Unitarian Universalist Association of Congregations.

09 08 07 06   8 7 6 5 4 3 2 1

This book is printed on acid-free paper that meets the uncoated paper
ANSI/NISO specifications for permanence as revised in 1992.

Composition by Wilsted & Taylor Publishing Services

Library of Congress Cataloging-in-Publication Data

Global values 101 : a short course / edited by Kate Holbrook . . . [et al.].—
1st ed.
      p. cm.
   Includes bibliographical references and index.
   ISBN 0-8070-0305-0 (pbk. : alk. paper) 1. Social values. 2. Social justice.
I. Title: Global values one hundred one. II. Title: Global values one hundred
one. III. Holbrook, Kate.

   HM681.G55   2005
   170'.973—dc22   2005013091

I arise in the morning torn between a desire to improve the world and a desire to enjoy the world. This makes it hard to plan the day.

—E. B. WHITE

CONTENTS

INTRODUCTION

Few college courses generate as much public attention and controversy as the one that led to this book. The *New York Times* called the course Idealism 101, and *Boston Magazine* wrote: "If Harvard's most popular course, Economics 10, prepares econ majors to become employee-axing, environment-wrecking CEOs, its *second* most popular course (and largest elective)... goes the other way, leading its students toward St. Francis–style sainthood." The course, the magazine continued, is "taught by the slim, wispy-voiced, and vaguely monkish Brian Palmer."

How did a course in the religion program, led by someone *Slate* magazine correctly described as an "obscure lecturer," attract international media coverage and as many as six hundred students per semester? To understand that turn of events, one can begin four years ago at a tent city that appeared in Harvard Yard.

During the neoliberal 1990s, Harvard subcontracted jobs and paid miserly wages to the people who mowed the lawns, mopped the floors, and cooked the potatoes. An employee at the world's wealthiest university could work full-time and be homeless at night.

Many students pleaded on these workers' behalf, but to no avail. Then, in April 2001, fifty students stormed into the Harvard president's office. They carried backpacks full of food and cell phones and announced that they would occupy the office until an adequate "Living Wage" was paid to the janitors and cooks.

The campus was electrified. Daily demonstrations took place outside the president's office, and dining-hall workers delivered free pizzas to the occupiers through the windows. Dozens of people began camping in tents in Harvard Yard, ready to bear witness at any hour if the police tried to remove the protesters by force.

Harvard's manicured lawns became a space of human connection as never before, complete with signs renaming the walkways after such figures as Mahatma Gandhi and Nelson Mandela. Coming home from my office in the evening, I would often encounter groups of students and workers discussing strategies or singing protest songs.

This went on for three weeks. The university's power holders —known as the Harvard Corporation—were increasingly embarrassed by the media coverage they received, with stories spotlighting the gap between golden-parachuted money managers and hard-knocks janitors. On Day 21, the corporation agreed to a process that would establish a Living Wage for the workers who sustain this preparatory school for tomorrow's elites. The alliance of workers, students, and teachers had won an astonishing victory.

In that atmosphere of engagement and hope, my students and I began to notice the injuries of inequality that secured our affluence. We interviewed cooks and cleaners and security guards. In a university fed by the donations of billionaires, we read Barbara Ehrenreich's words about a different kind of philanthropy. The working poor, she wrote, are "the major philanthropists of our society. They neglect their own children so that the children of others will be cared for; they live in substandard housing so that other homes will be shiny and perfect; they endure privation so that inflation will be low and stock prices will be high. To be a member of the working poor is to be an anonymous donor, a nameless benefactor, to everyone else."

These concerns became the central theme of my courses and thereby of this book: How are we to live in a world of gaping inequalities? What are we to do when other people are being hurt? What are the obligations of those who are comfortable to those who suffer?

The Living Wage struggle had prompted me and many of my students to examine what the late Susan Sontag called "the inadequacy of our response to the simultaneity of wildly contrasting human fates." She remembered the philosopher Voltaire: "Hearing the news of the earthquake that leveled Lisbon on Nov. 1, 1755 . . . the great Voltaire was struck by our inveterate inability to take in what happened elsewhere. 'Lisbon lies in ruins,' Voltaire wrote, 'and here in Paris we dance.'" Or here in Harvard Square.

One of my graduate students, Kate Holbrook, and I planned a new course to address how one might live in such a world. What does it mean to live deliberately, as Henry David Thoreau once put it? How can one "make a difference"? The course was to be called Personal Choice and Global Transformation, and it was set to begin on September 12, 2001.

On September 11, as my mother's kitchen rattled when the second plane struck the World Trade Center and my brother-in-law evacuated a day-care center at the Pentagon, I wondered what my students needed to hear and what I was capable of saying at a time when we all felt overwhelmed and heartbroken.

The next day, I organized my lecture around a diary entry by the former UN secretary general Dag Hammarskjöld: "God has a use for you, even though what He asks doesn't happen to suit you at the moment." On that day of smoldering ashes, many of us felt that the world might have a use for us, the world might need our services, in ways that we did not intend or wish for.

Just then, students in fields ranging from computer science to botany to law shared a common interest in influencing a world gone wrong. As enrollment in my course swelled during the following days, we had to move the class four times to larger and larger lecture halls.

My teaching philosophy began with the recognition that neither I nor anyone else had definitive answers to the ethical and political questions we were exploring. Before each semester, Kate and I scheduled a dozen or more individuals to visit the course for in-class interviews. These persons ranged from janitors to billionaires, from professors to corporate CEOs to nuns. They shared only a seriousness about the need to confront the world's violence and injustice.

Our guests did not give any lectures. Instead, the students read work by or about them (*lecture* in French means "reading"). Groups of students prepared questions in advance and posed them during the interviews. Kate and I trotted about the auditorium with portable microphones, periodically intervening with comments and questions of our own.

Students found this format enlivening. They often sought to press our guests—to take up difficult issues that seemed to have been overlooked or evaded in the articles we read. At other times the focus was on the preparation and thought that had enabled our visitors to make difficult personal choices, such as the decision to become a whistle-blower or to work in a war zone. Student reflections continued after each interview, in discussion sections, daily writing assignments, Web-based exchanges, and weekly class dinners in Harvard dining halls.

For the guests, the experience of being grilled by a group of energetic young people was often profound and vivifying. One guest, Robert Reich, credits his course visit with tipping the scales for his decision—made later the same day—to run for governor of Massachusetts. (To the disappointment of students who flocked to his campaign, he didn't get the job.)

Some interviews moved students and guests alike to tears, as when a Harvard dining-hall worker spoke of the love she feels toward the people she serves. Other days were tragicomic: a seminude guest from an animal-rights organization staged an antifur protest in Harvard Square, only to miss his interview while under arrest for indecent exposure. And interviews could occasionally become tense, as when Harvard's president, Lawrence Summers, bristled at a student's question about why the college gives an automatic advantage in admissions to the children of its alumni.

In selecting interviews for inclusion in the pages that follow, my coeditors and I looked for material of enduring significance, beyond the particular place and time of the course. Some discussions were left out because they were tied to specific moments, such as the run-up to the invasion of Iraq. Others were too Harvard-centric to be of broader interest. And some guests did not want their interviews to be published.

What remains is a set of sixteen conversations, each one full of idiosyncratic formulations as students and guests struggle to say what they mean. It is that rough-hewn quality that makes the texts captivating. Lacking professional caution and PR polish, these interviews have an openhearted quality, admitting weaknesses and suggesting that the conversation is not finished.

As the thirteenth-century saint Albertus Magnus put it, "The greatest of all human pleasures is to seek the truth in conversation." My colleagues and I hope that the conversations in this book will spark many others.

BRIAN C. W. PALMER
Stockholm, Sweden
June 2005

1. HISTORY AND INVESTIGATIONS
Asking the Questions

HOWARD ZINN, historian

The son of a working-class family, Howard Zinn had his political consciousness ignited after serving as a unionized shipyard worker and later as an air force pilot during World War II. As an activist, writer, and teacher, he has been the voice of dissent ever since. Professor emeritus of political science at Boston University, Zinn is the recipient of the Thomas Merton, Eugene V. Debs, and Lannan Foundation Awards. The author of more than twenty books, he is best known for his powerful memoir, You Can't Be Neutral on a Moving Train: A Personal History of Our Times, *and* A People's History of the United States: 1492– Present, *which traces American history through marginalized voices and has sold more than one million copies. In this interview, Zinn relates personal and historical anecdotes to illustrate the inner workings of democracy. He also proposes differing visions of the history of U.S. warfare, the American soldier, and the American Dream.*

Question: In your book *You Can't Be Neutral Moving on a Moving Train,* you discuss how we are all susceptible to changing attitudes and beliefs. Can you describe a time when you experienced a change in attitudes and beliefs, and what sparked that change?

Howard Zinn: You mean I have to admit that I was not born with all the wonderful ideas that I now have, that I changed at a certain point? I went to this demonstration in Times Square—in the book, I sort of dramatize this a little, exaggerate, lie—and that was a point at which an important view of mine changed. I was a teenager growing up in a working-class neighborhood with sort of liberal ideas that were vaguely antiwar and anti–bad things. I had read Upton Sinclair and Jack London and Dickens and so on, but I still had certain illusions about American democracy, and how, when things are bad, it is because they are deviations from a fundamental democratic notion. I still had the idea that there are evil forces and good forces, and then there is the government in between; the government is a neutral arbiter. When you are growing up, you like to think of policemen as neutral. So I went to this demonstration, which was a vaguely Communist demonstration. I didn't know. I swear, I didn't know! Please, tell everybody I didn't know it was a Communist demonstration. At a certain point, a mounted officer attacked this peaceful demonstration, and soon after, I was smacked by a policeman, by either his fist or a club, and I was knocked unconscious. Then, when I woke up—now I am overdramatizing this—the sky cleared.

It suddenly occurred to me: police do not attack peaceful demonstrations. After all, we have a bill of rights, freedom of speech, and freedom of assembly. But they were attacking all these people. It occurred to me that the government is not neutral; the government is generally on the side of privilege and power, and the Bill of Rights has only as much meaning as whoever has power to enforce it or ignore it. That was a turning point, you might say, from being a liberal to being a radical. A liberal still has some faith in the goodwill of the system: the U.S. really doesn't mean to do ill in Iraq, we all have good intentions, we had good intentions in Vietnam, it was just a mistake, as McNamara would say. A radical says, "No, the truth is they do not have good intentions, their interests are different than most of the people."

I will point to one other turning point, which is connected, because I must have still harbored some innocence about the role of government. I taught at Spelman College, a black women's college in Atlanta, from 1956 to 1963, and I became involved in the movement there. Sometimes you know something vaguely, but then it is brought home to you powerfully. What was brought home to me powerfully was that you could not depend on the government or the Constitution if you had some deep grievance with the society. If there is some serious problem in the society, it is not going to be solved by the initiative of the government or by what the law says; it is going to come from what the people themselves do. That came from watching the presumably liberal federal government of Kennedy and Johnson not willing to do anything to enforce the Fourteenth and Fifteenth Amendments of the Constitution until the black people in the South rose up to do it by themselves. They got out and they protested and they went to jail and they got beaten and some of them got killed, and they created a commotion in the nation—and in the world— that finally caused the government of Kennedy and Johnson to begin to move in the direction of ending racial segregation. For me, this was a lesson in democracy. Democracy is what the people do; it is not what the government does.

Question: In *You Can't Be Neutral on a Moving Train* you write about how the situation in the United States today requires not just a new president or new laws but an uprooting of the old order, the introduction of a new kind of society. You write about a classless society of true democracy and true freedom, one that provides at least the most basic necessities: food, housing, and health care. These are ideals that very few people would disagree with, yet it seems difficult to find examples of countries and societies today, or even throughout history, that fit these ideals. Could you give us examples of a society today or in history that you believe other societies should emulate?

HZ: Usually that question comes in a slightly different form. After I have said something very critical about the United States, which I occasionally do, the question is usually a very truculent one: well, where else would you like to live? Once, after I had given a talk at some high school assembly, a student who was obviously not very happy with what I had said asked, "Why do you live in this country?" Good question. Are there any societies that I would be happier with? There are no societies in the world that are ideal, so the question is very complex.

There are things about the United States, obviously, which are very good. We have freedom of speech in this country to an extent that most countries in the world do not have, although we also have limitations on that freedom, which have to do with money and power and media control. We have a standard of living in this country, at least for the middle classes, that is higher than the standard of living in most places in the world, but you have to leave out the bottom forty million people in the population from that description. There are countries that have better social programs than we do. There are countries that have universal free medical care, which we do not have, leaving forty million of our people without health insurance. There are countries that have better unemployment benefits and more subsidized housing. There are countries where the difference between the rich and the poor is not as stark as it is in this country. But there is no system, no country in the world that I can point to as ideal.

I can think of two times in history when people created societies that seem to me worth emulating. One of these was in the few months of the Paris Commune in 1871. For a brief time in 1871, the Paris Commune had something very close to a real democracy. Decisions were made in democratic forums all over Paris, and the members of the Commune—that is, the representatives, the leaders—established that they would get no wage higher than that of the average worker in Paris. Try that with our senators and congressmen. It was a situation where the theater was free, where culture flourished. It was a remarkably democratic society for a few months—I guess too democratic—so it was crushed by the French army coming in from Versailles.

The other model is Catalonia in the first months of the Spanish Civil War. If you read George Orwell's *Homage to Catalonia* —he was in the Spanish Civil War—he describes what happens when the anarchists took over Barcelona. The phrase "took over" does not exactly fit the idea of anarchists, but anarchism, you might say, flourished in Barcelona for about six months in the early years of the Spanish Civil War. Orwell describes how in this remarkably egalitarian society, people shared things, and there was virtually no crime because people had the things they needed or could get the things they needed by exchanging goods and services with other people. It was a peaceful society until the forces from the outside moved in to destroy it.

We would have to pick and choose from among good societies in the world to find an ideal society. In the United States, as I said, there are lots of things you can point to which are good, but we need some serious correcting before we have a good society. It is particularly shameful that we have such a gross national product—it is gross in that it is used for purposes that do not advance human needs. Much of GNP goes to the military budget, and much of the wealth is siphoned off into the upper 1 percent of the population. With the great resources, wealth, talent that we have in the United States, we could really create an ideal society, but we have not so far.

Question: You wrote, "I've always resented the smug statements of politicians of how in America, if you worked hard, you would become rich." Many of us believe this. We have always been told that if we work hard, we will succeed. Do you not believe in this ethic of the American Dream?

HZ: No. I do not believe in the fantasy—I don't even want to call it a dream—that there is some necessary relationship between how hard you work and how prosperous and successful you are. Sure, there are people who work hard and become successful. Sometimes there is a relationship; often there isn't. The point is that there is no necessary relationship. A lot also depends on what you consider work. Sometimes people think that the president of the university works fifty times as hard as the janitor at the university. I don't think so. Society certainly does not reward people with material benefits on the basis of how hard they work. A typical CEO in the sixties had an income about forty times the income of the average American worker. Today it is four hundred times. It is ridiculous; how hard does a CEO work?

I think of people who are nurses, social workers, elementary or high school teachers. I think of people who work hard doing very useful things, and they barely have enough money to get by. I think of artists and musicians and actors and poets who have such a hard time in this free-market society. The market dooms people like that to a subsistence living.

Whether you become prosperous or not does not depend on how hard you work or how smart you are. How do you calculate smartness? Do you go by IQ tests? Some people are smart at

things that make a lot of money, and others are smart at things
that do not make a lot of money. Certainly there is no correlation
between how prosperous or materially successful you become
and what contribution you make to society. All you have to do is
look at the fortunes that are made by people who produced poi-
sons or nuclear weapons.

Question: In an article for the *Boston Globe,* "The Case against the
War in Iraq," you write that President Bush's doctrine of preemptive war should be the focus of a national debate "far beyond
the limited vision of the Capitol and the White House." However, as you point out in *You Can't Be Neutral on a Moving Train,*
many people in the United States today continue to work multiple jobs simply to put food on the table. How can we expect citizens living in poverty to actively participate in democracy when
they do not have the time, resources, or energy necessary to consider national issues?

HZ: There is no doubt what you are suggesting is true. People who
have to spend a lot of their time just working to survive are going to have a more difficult time participating. It is very clear
that 50 percent of potential voters do not vote in presidential
elections, and those people are predominantly people at the
lower income levels. This suggests, for one, that they are too con-
sumed with their own problems—maybe working two jobs or
three jobs to keep the family going—to participate in the political process. Second, precisely because of the conditions that
they live under—and they have lived under those conditions
whether the Democrats or Republicans are in power—they
have the feeling that voting is not really going to help them
whichever party gets in power. The people at that level, the people who are working very hard to make a living, are out of the po-

litical process, a process in which, even if they did participate, the results would be very limited.

Yet this is not a static situation. We have to expand the idea of political participation beyond the idea of electoral politics. In the fifties and sixties, when black people went out into the streets and demonstrated and protested and sat in and created a commotion in the country, they were participating in the political process even if they did not vote—and in the South, most of them were unable to vote. So political participation is open to people in the low-income groups or people of color who have been shut out in one way or another; they can participate, but they do not do it through electoral politics. Similarly, workers who feel exploited and want to change their working conditions may not participate in electoral politics, but they may organize unions, go on strike, conduct boycotts, and in that way they are participating in a political process which historically has proved more important than voting.

Question: How were you so convinced of the mission of World War II, enough to leave your family and wife behind, potentially sacrificing your life? What dangers do you see now in this so-called blind faith in a cause?

HZ: I volunteered for the air force in World War II because I had been reading about fascism, Mussolini, Hitler, and I had been watching in the newspapers the sweep of Hitler across Europe. It became clear to me that this was a cause that was worth fighting for: the defeat of fascism. I wanted to play a part in that and volunteered for the air force. After the end of the war, I began to think that even this good war, this best of wars, had to be reconsidered in moral terms; it was more complex than simply a good war. There were all sorts of facts that had to be taken into account in assessing this war, and even if you took them all into account, there is no assessment that could make it *simply* a good war.

When my crew and I finished our bombing missions in Europe, the war in Europe was over, but the war with Japan was still going on, so we flew the plane that we had been bombing with back to the United States and then had a thirty-day furlough. After that, we would be going on to the Pacific to drop bombs on Japan. On this thirty-day furlough, my wife and I decided that we would take an excursion into the country. We stopped at a bus stop and saw the newspaper, the headline of which read, "Atomic Bomb Dropped on Hiroshima." I remember both of us thinking, "Good!" But I had no idea what the atomic bomb was; I just knew it was a bigger bomb and would probably bring the war to an end. "Great, I don't have to go to the Pacific." But I had no idea what the atomic bomb was or what it did. Then, after the war, I read John Hersey's book *Hiroshima.* What John Hersey did was go to Hiroshima after the blast and talk to the survivors —people who were blind, people without legs or arms, people whose skin you could not look at. Suddenly, the human results of aerial bombing came to me in a way that had never occurred while I was dropping bombs. When you are dropping bombs from thirty thousand feet—keep this in mind when you hear these nice stories of pilots coming back from bombing missions in Afghanistan and Iraq—you do not see people, you do not hear screams, you do not see mangled limbs on children. This is modern warfare. That is why you can see a marine in Iraq carrying a sign saying, "We killed twenty-six today; it was a good day." Twenty-six *who*? Twenty-six *what*?

I thought about a mission I had flown at the very end of the war. The war was over, in effect, except that they sent us over to bomb a little town on the Atlantic coast of France because there were twenty thousand German soldiers who were there, not doing anything, not bothering anybody, just waiting for the war to end. Somebody up there decided that they would send twelve hundred heavy bombers over to this little town of Lyon, dropping a new kind of bomb which they called jelly gasoline—napalm. This was the first use of napalm in the European theater. You know by now what napalm is and what it does to human beings. I thought nothing of it at the time. I had no thought of getting up in the briefing room, saying, "Why are we doing this? The war is over. Why are we dropping more bombs, killing more people?" We ended up killing several thousand Germans, several thousand French. More medals, more experience with a new type of bomb. This is warfare, even in a good war.

Anyway, I began to rethink the whole question of war, even the best of wars. The worst thing about World War II is that it is now used as a metaphor for every other war. The good war becomes a sort of basis of casting its moral glow over every ugly war we have fought since.

I want to answer your question about how to overcome blind loyalty—and it is blind loyalty. You enter the military and you don't think; you do your job. I understand how ordinary people can commit atrocities in warfare. Ordinary guys can go up there, drop bombs, kill women and children; it is just doing your job. You make one judgment at the very beginning of your participation in the war, the judgment that I am on the right side. There is Hitler or Saddam Hussein. Once you make that decision—they are the bad guys, we are the good guys—you don't have to think anymore. No more judgments have to be made, no more reconsideration. You have already decided everything, and at that point, you can do whatever you want without thinking about it. That is how you get the bombing of civilians in enormous numbers in Dresden, a hundred thousand dead in Tokyo in one night, Hiroshima and Nagasaki.

I see this painful scene on television where they talk to a young GI in Iraq. "Why are you here?" "Well, I feel that I owe this to my country." Really, how do you know you are doing this for your country? You are doing this for your government. There is a difference between your government and your country. Just read the Declaration of Independence, the basic democratic document. The government is an artificial creation set up to achieve equality, life, liberty, and the pursuit of happiness. The government can violate that, and if it violates that, it is not fulfilling its charge, and you the people, according to the Declaration of Independence, have the right to overthrow or abolish the government. If you have the right to overthrow or abolish the government, you have the right to disobey it.

There are a number of things to do to prevent people from becoming blind followers of the march to war, blind followers of a process that ends up in the killing of large numbers of ordinary people. The thousands and thousands of Iraqis we have killed are not Saddam Hussein. We did not kill Saddam Hussein. When you make a war against a tyrant, you kill the victims of the tyrant. There is a lot of education to be done, especially among high school and college students, about disobedience to government. Read Thoreau's essay "Civil Disobedience." Read the history of the Vietnam War. History is very important. Read the history of wars and the history of foreign policy—not only our wars, because we are just the last of the imperialist powers (at least I hope we are the last)—and you can never again believe the president of the United States when he comes before the public and says, "We have got to fight this war, we are in danger, it is for national security, I am here to defend you, it is a war against terrorism," and all that crap, really. You might not know definitively that he is lying, because maybe this is a break from history. Governments have lied again and again, from the Mexican War, the Spanish-American War, the Korean War, Vietnam War, the Panama War, Grenada War, the Gulf War. But this time they are telling the truth. Maybe. But you would start out in skepticism; you would not rush to believe the president. There is a lot of education to be done about history, about the meaning of democracy, about the meaning of patriotism.

Question: Many critics of the war in Iraq emphasize the role that the United States played in supporting Saddam Hussein in the Iran-Iraq War and also the U.S. failure to acknowledge the genocidal attacks on Kurds in northern Iraq. Given past transgressions in the Gulf region, doesn't the U.S. bear some responsibility in trying to fix its mistakes, even if it is fifteen years too late?

HZ: Let me get your question straight. The fact that in 1986–87 the United States supported Saddam Hussein by giving him chemical and biological agents means that the United States bears a responsibility to make up for that support of Hussein by now getting rid of him? If the object of the United States were to create a democratic Iraq and to do it without a war, well, we might at least consider it. But so much of what you decide is right or wrong in Iraq depends on your estimate of the motives of the United States. Given the history of the United States, not just the history of what we did to support Saddam Hussein, not just the history of giving him chemical and biological weapons, but given the history of the United States in its foreign policy, it is very dubious that now we are trying to do the right thing and we are trying to create a democratic Iraq.

I suggest that what the Bush administration is doing is drawing an iron curtain around Iraq and Saddam Hussein and asking that the American citizenry focus only on Iraq and only on Saddam Hussein. Focus on what weapons of mass destruction we might possibly someday discover. Focus on Saddam Hussein as a tyrant, which he is, of course. Focus on his misdeeds of the past —"misdeeds" is a euphemism, of course, for torture and imprisonment and so forth. Focus only on that. That is what they would like us to do.

But I suggest that if you broaden your view geographically and historically, then you would be very, very dubious that the United States really wants to make up for what it did in the 1980s. Because the problem is not just making up for what it did in the 1980s. The problem is that there is a long history in American foreign policy which goes beyond giving Saddam Hussein his weapons of mass destruction in the 1980s; there is a long history of the United States giving deadly weapons to military dictatorships all over the world and collaborating in the annihilation of people by tyrants in Asia, Africa, and Latin America. The history of American support of military juntas and death squads is so odious that it would be very hard for me to believe that at this point the United States simply wants to make up for the sin that it committed in Iraq in the 1980s. It has many, many more sins to make up for.

The history of the United States suggests that making up for sins is not its aim. Its aims are the aims of empire. If you look beyond the particular situation in Iraq on which they want us to focus alone, if you look at the history of the United States, it is a history of expansion—the expansion of political and military and economic power—from the American Revolution on. It started with the obliteration of the line that the English set west of the colonies, saying in the Proclamation of 1763 that you cannot go into Indian territory. Then after winning the Revolution, the Americans moved westward in what was called gently, I remember in high school history classes, Westward Expansion, a euphemism for annihilating and removing the Indian tribes that lived on the continent. That expansion through the nineteenth century included instigating a war with Mexico and taking half of Mexico, then moving into the Caribbean at the turn of the century and pretending to liberate Cuba from Spain. The United States freed Cuba from Spain but not from us. Spain was out, the United States was in. We instituted American banks, American corporations, American railroads, and American military bases in Cuba, and also rewrote the Cuban constitution to allow military intervention at any time. We so often pretended to liberate, operating under names like "Operation Iraqi Freedom" and "Operation Just Cause" for our invasion into Panama.

There is a pattern of imperial wars, like the present war. The pattern is a very powerful military nation going into a nation that is "backward" and that really has no defenses, and that is true of Iraq today. It is not really a war. It is a slaughter. That is what it was in the Philippines at the start of the twentieth century, and about eight hundred thousand people died. After the victory over Spain in Cuba, the U.S. sent an army into the Philippines, and unlike the "splendid little war," as it was called in Cuba, this war lasted for years against the Filipinos who wanted independence. That pattern of expansion continued with the marines going into Central America again and again, and it continued with a long occupation of Haiti and the Dominican Republic starting after World War I. After World War II, the U.S. makes a deal with Saudi Arabia with Ibn Saud about taking over the domination of the oil fields of the Middle East in return for keeping this monarch in power. The expansion has continued down to the present day; we have one hundred military bases in a hundred different countries and our warships on every sea. This history of the United States' power suggests that our motives for going into Iraq have really nothing to do with redressing a wrong, one wrong among so many in the world.

Question: You have argued that the United States should pull back from being a military superpower and should instead become a humanitarian superpower. What would you say in cases such as Rwanda and Kosovo, where world opinion demanded U.S. intervention and humanitarian aid was impossible without military support? Is military force sometimes necessary for humanitarian goals?

HZ: Good question. Definition of a good question: one that you cannot answer. Well, I will do my best. That is a question that is not easy to answer because fundamentally I am against war; I am against military action. I do not call myself a pacifist because the term "pacifist" suggests an absolute prohibition against any kind of military action under any circumstances, and I do not want to be absolute about anything. I want to leave the way open for the possibility, and it is only a possibility, that at certain points in history—and they are not too frequent—it may be useful, it may be morally acceptable for a *small* focused use of force to prevent an enormous catastrophe. That was the situation in Rwanda. In Rwanda, the show of force by a small UN contingent—a contingent that was withdrawn at a critical point with the United States playing a very key and very bad role in withdrawing it— might have saved huge numbers of lives from the genocide.

I point to another situation. One of Bill Clinton's few decent moves in foreign policy was when he sent a military force to Haiti not to wage war but really to push a military junta out of power and bring Aristide, who had been the popular elected leader of Haiti, back in power. Those are situations in which a small, focused use of force to prevent some large catastrophe might be justifiable.

Kosovo is a more complicated issue. In Kosovo it was not a matter of a small and focused use of force. It was a large and un-differentiated use of force in which we bombed not very specific aggressive targets, but rather, we bombed major cities and civil-ian populations in order to achieve something for Kosovo which might very well have been achieved by diplomatic efforts. To get the details on that, read Noam Chomsky's book *The New Military Humanism: Lessons from Kosovo.* There was a humanitar-ian catastrophe in Kosovo, but I think that indiscriminate use of force probably made things worse instead of better. And there was probably another solution. There are times when you could conceivably suggest military force to solve something, but where diplomatic possibilities exist which are not taken, and they are generally not taken because the intervening powers really would prefer to make war.

I think of the war in Korea, which does not meet my criteria of a just war. The war in Korea was a massive use of military force, so massive that several million people were killed in Ko-rea because North Korea had invaded South Korea, although there is a lot of dispute over who provoked whom. However, it was a situation that could have been resolved by diplomacy. There were, in fact, attempts to solve it by diplomacy, which the United States rejected in the first few months of the war, and so the war went on for three years. At the end of that time, where were we? Exactly where we were before: dictatorship in North Korea, dictatorship in South Korea, and in the meantime, several more million people were dead. Leaving an opening for the possible use of focused, small, military force to prevent a great catastrophe should not be easily moved over into a situation that does not meet those criteria.

Certainly the present war in Iraq and most of the wars that we have fought since World War II do not meet those criteria.

Question: In *A People's History of the United States,* you frequently present history from the standpoint of so-called losers or people who have had no voice in the history books. From whose vantage point would you present the historical events that are taking place today in the U.S. or abroad? That is, who do you think are the losers and what do they have to say?

HZ: I would certainly look at this war in Iraq from the standpoint of the GIs, the American GIs. People say, "Now that we are at war, we have to support the GIs." Absolutely. I can think of two ways that you are not supporting the GIs. One way that you are not supporting the GIs is by sending them to die. The other way you are not supporting the GIs is that when they come back, you treat them as if they are not really human beings. Already the Bush administration is cutting veterans' benefits. I would also look at the war from the standpoint of what kind of sicknesses the GIs are going to encounter in this war. In the first Gulf war in 1991, only a few hundred soldiers actually died, but hundreds of thousands of veterans came back with sicknesses that the Veterans Administration is not acknowledging but which teams of doctors have said are real. In the Spanish-American War in Cuba, the United States lost only a few hundred people in battle in Cuba, but several thousand died due to poisoned meat that was bought from the packinghouses of Chicago and given to the soldiers, meat that had been left over from the Civil War. What I am suggesting is that we ought to look not only at the casualties but at what the GIs experience in Iraq. For example, we ought to look at the effects of depleted uranium used in weapons, which has been shown to have very, very deadly effects on people exposed to it. There is something about war in which it is not only the enemy that gets hurt, but your side gets hurt by the technological means that you use to destroy the enemy. So, yes, I would look at the war from the standpoint of these Americans who are suffering in the war.

I would also look at the war from the standpoint of the so-called enemy, the other side. Now Saddam Hussein is not a so-called enemy. He *is* an enemy. But the people of Iraq are not. I would look at the war from the standpoint of the ordinary Iraqi civilians who are dying. We are not getting an accurate picture in the American press of how much suffering is going on in Iraq, of how many people are dying in Iraq. You have to look at the foreign press in order to get the stories of how many civilian deaths we have caused in our bombing, how many so-called accidents have taken place, how many families have been wiped out by our bombing, how many neighborhoods have been destroyed. At the end of the first Gulf war, Colin Powell was saying rather proudly that only a few hundred Americans had died. A reporter asked him, "Well what about the Iraqi dead?" And he said—and this is a fairly close thing to a quote—he said, "That is not a matter I am terribly concerned with," and in general that is considered a matter that we Americans are not supposed to be terribly concerned with. So, I would certainly look at the war not only from the standpoint of American suffering but from the standpoint of the so-called enemy.

I would not simply talk about the innocent civilians but also innocent soldiers: the soldiers on both sides are innocent. American soldiers, Iraqi soldiers. Who are they? You know, I was in the military. I know who joins the military. The American soldiers, the Iraqi soldiers, the young people who join the military for one reason or another—they did not join to kill other people. They are only vaguely aware of what in the world the war is being fought about. They are not given lessons in their military training on American imperialism; that would be asking a little too much. The soldiers on both sides are conscripts or volunteers, but they are the innocent ones sent to war by the leaders of their country, whether from Iraq or the United States.

I would also look at the war from the standpoint of those Americans whose benefits are being cut by the enormous sums of money being given to the military apparatus. Among the cuts proposed in the recent Bush budget were cuts in free school lunches for kids. I thought that was really interesting. Obviously, there are kids who are getting free school lunches who should not be getting them, and we ought to seek them out and take away those lunches. That is what we are about to do.

Question: In your article "Growing Up Class Conscious," you explain that even when you moved out of a world of just scraping by, never having enough, bringing your children to free medical clinics, even when you received your proper degrees and became a college professor, you never forgot that way of life and you never stopped being class conscious. How do you suggest that those who come from more privileged backgrounds live both socially conscious and socially responsible lives?

HZ: I suppose my present class consciousness comes at least partly out of my own background, but people with different class backgrounds also are class conscious. So I cannot ask you to rework your background, right? But whoever you are and whatever your background, you are a person of relatively free will. Therefore, you are a person who is capable of looking at the world, at the distribution of wealth, at the distribution of power and deciding in what way you can intercede and help the situation and help redress the grievances of people in this country who have to work too hard for much too little.

I remember a few years ago, there was a situation in a factory just north of Boston, immigrant women workers in a curtain factory, and ten of them were fired for trying to organize a union because the conditions were absolutely abominable. Well, people from all over the community came to support them: students at Harvard and other colleges, members of the Teamsters Union, people from churches—it didn't matter what their class background was. They all gathered in one place and demonstrated and walked into the office of the owner of the factory and would not leave until certain demands were met. And so about thirteen of us were arrested for refusing to leave, and four days later the employer capitulated and rehired those people who had been fired. But that was an example of people of varying class backgrounds joining in solidarity to do something about economic inequities in society.

So I think, yes, that is something everybody can do. Nobody

need feel trapped by their money or their parents' money or the jobs that they have. We all have the capacity to break out of whatever restrictions our class status puts us in and do what we think is right.

ELAINE SCARRY, literary scholar

Though established in the academic world as a scholar of English literature, Elaine Scarry is widely known for her investigations of torture, war, nuclear weapons, and citizenship. Her reading list ranges from Virginia Woolf to Aviation Week and Space Technology, *and her own work contributes to multiple fields. Her books include the classic* The Body in Pain: The Making and Unmaking of the World, On Beauty and Being Just, *and* Dreaming by the Book. *She has undertaken studies of 9-11, airplane crashes, and the Patriot Act while also helping to formulate Ethiopia's constitution. The holder of a distinguished professorship at Harvard, Scarry received the 2000 Truman Capote Award for Literary Criticism and the National Book Critics' Circle Award, among others. In this interview, she explores the obligations of citizenship and the uses of critical thinking in seeking justice for humankind.*

Question: Not every professor of English reads *Aviation Week and Space Technology,* and not everyone grapples with pressing human problems of war and torture. Can you tell us something about how you became such an engaged and serious citizen?

Elaine Scarry: The thing that should be explained is why people do *not* read across many fields, rather than why people do. Students like yourselves go from one kind of intellectual path to another in the course of the day. You might have a math class at 10:00 in the morning, then you might have a literature class at 2:00 in the afternoon, a philosophy course at 3:00, and a physics class at 5:00. That kind of work across different disciplines is, to my mind, more likely to produce clear thinking. In fact, John Locke, who wrote *The Second Treatise of Government,* once said, "The surest way to stop thinking is to read books only in one field and talk only to people who work in one field." Part of the way one continues to think is to look across fields. The reason for that is when you are working within one field, none of the large framing questions are usually disputed or in question, whereas when you keep passing back and forth across different fields, you have to keep tripping over the threshold of the assumptions in any one field. You are more likely to see perils in them or weaknesses in them as well as strengths, and see some of the large framing questions.

But your question had another part, which is social engagement. Nothing about being an English professor exempts me from the obligation to attend to what is going on in the country. Nothing about being a taxi driver would exempt me from the obligation, and nothing about being a teacher does. If you are in the position of knowing how to do research and read texts, then your obligation goes up a bit because it means that you know how to track down information that might be of assistance in deliberating about certain issues.

Question: Could you comment about how your study of literature has helped shape your sociopolitical beliefs? How has it changed the way you approach questions of modern-day life and politics?

ES: The work that I originally did on physical pain and the difficulty of expressing physical pain was first brought to my attention by reading literature. The reason it was brought to my attention was that I did not find many examples there of physical pain. That was startling to me as a young student because I thought of literature as something that could address the most obvious dilemmas that we are all in, such as falling in love or losing a friend, and also the most esoteric of problems. I wondered how it could possibly be the case that one does not find many examples of physical pain in literature. Is it that there is some kind of taboo, or does it come from the inherent difficulty of expression? I later learned that Virginia Woolf had a very fine formulation of this same observation. She said, "The merest school girl when she falls in love has Shakespeare or Keats to speak her mind for her. But just let someone get a headache and language at once runs dry." In this case, it was knowing that literature was the best companion we can have on many problems, and yet it was not there in this one situation, that led me to look not only at literary but also at other contexts where people have tried to invent the language: physicians, Amnesty International, people writing about war, and so on.

The other thing that I would say about literature is partly addressed in my essay "The Difficulty of Imagining Other Persons." Literature is not sufficient for the work of trying to imagine other people, whether it is people in Iraq or people who live on the other side of town or people who are on the night shift when you are on the day shift. I do not think literature alone can enable us to be mindful of all these other people because our imaginations are not strong enough. But literature in combination with certain very sensible practices, such as having laws that we agree to follow, works well to make us more mindful of other people and does so in part by making us aware of the limits in our ability to imagine other people. I cite the writings of Thomas Hardy, the nineteenth-century novelist, and the way in which he lets us feel the weight of one of his heroines or one of his heroes, and then lets us watch the other characters subtract from that person until they become nothing more than a piece of gossip or a rumor, and we feel the pain of that diminution. Now that is what happens when you are trying to imagine one other person. What happens when you are trying to imagine eighty thousand people, or what happens when you are trying to imagine five million people? We are always coming up against the limits of our own imaginations.

Question: What is the value of literature in ethical and political discussions?

ES: Brilliant people have written about this, including the philosopher Martha Nussbaum and the philosopher Richard Rorty. Their articles would be well worth reading because rather than starting out as people who read literature, they start as people who are philosophers who then go to literature for models that often accommodate some of the messiness and liquidity of our interactions with one another. There are many different ways of answering that question. There is a specific problem with literature that is summarized by the poet Auden in a poem he wrote as an elegy for Yeats: "Poetry makes nothing happen: / It survives / In the valley of its saying." But at the end of that poem, he steps back and acknowledges that maybe poetry does make something happen. We know that there are only a small number of literary works that have themselves brought about large, concrete changes. I cite a couple of them in that article on "The Difficulty of Imagining Other Persons." *Uncle Tom's Cabin* had huge political consequences for the grave problem of slavery. A more debatable case is *A Passage to India* by E. M. Forster, which, according to the poet Stephen Spender, overnight caused people in Britain to begin to think of their colonial relation to India very differently than they had before. But using those two pieces of literature would be misleading because they represent exceptional cases where poems or novels really have changed a whole nation's way of perceiving things.

I have tried to argue in a book called *On Beauty and Being Just* that beauty and philosophic discussions of justice often work together in that both of them take injury as the thing that they are opposed to. In my own work, I have sometimes found that things that I am trying to argue for using only legal arguments have been more successful when other people have used arguments from beauty. It might take a while to unfold that, but I can at least give you just a thumbnail sketch.

For about ten years, I have been working on a book about the way in which we have given up our own laws that are supposed to protect us at the moment when we go to war. One of those laws is that we have to have a congressional declaration of war. Since World War II, we have not had any congressional declaration of war: not in Korea, not in Vietnam, not for various invasions. In the Gulf War in the early nineties we had a conditional declaration, which many constitutional scholars have seen as not an actual declaration of war. We also have a rule, the right to bear arms, which is meant to distribute authorization to a wide population for making decisions about whether we go to war. My concern is the kind of weapons of mass destruction that our own country has and the way in which these are incompatible with our laws. Recognizing that such weapons are incompatible with our laws matters because the laws then give us the tools for calling back the power and getting rid of those weapons—if we would just use those tools. Once laws are given up, however, the lost laws never seem like something vibrant and vital, something disastrous to have given up. I feel that people seem not to mind the fact that our Constitution is just being torn up. When you think of the kind of injuries that are involved in nuclear war, it may seem beside the point to say that a social contract was torn up. But I want to turn that around and say, "That is what it looks like when you tear up a social contract: those images we know of widespread and massive injury. That is what it looks like when you tear up a social contract."

When I ask myself who has been successful on this issue, I think it is people who have explicitly or implicitly made an argument about beauty. For example, you may know the book by Jonathan Schell *The Fate of the Earth,* which had a big influence on public concern about nuclear weapons when it first came out. Though Schell's argument in *The Fate of the Earth* really was incredibly politically knowledgeable, it was also an argument about the beauty of the earth and about the membrane of our own eyes and the eyes of other creatures that would be made blind by the first flashes of light, and about algae swimming in the oceans, and about a kind of membrane that we produce with our own breath that becomes part of the larger ecosystem of the earth. Rachel Carson's *Silent Spring* is another instance of a book that, by reminding people of the beauty of the world, brought about concrete changes in people's actions and habits. Even if we only occasionally come upon works like *Uncle Tom's Cabin* or *A Passage to India* that we can watch bringing about a revolution in perception, works of literature that keep us in touch with the beauty of the world always act to bring us into contact with our best selves and act to make us opposed to injury.

Question: As you just mentioned, one of the suggestions that you discuss in "The Difficulty of Imagining Other Persons" for getting past the imagination impediment is changing our lives. What do you think we can do to change our relationship with people that are not part of our nation and can't be influenced by our lives, specifically the Iraqi people today?

ES: It is important to find ways of practicing symmetrical thinking, and the piece that you read, "A Nuclear Double Standard," provides an example of our tendency to think nonsymmetrically. They have one weapon under way and not yet made. We have thousands of weapons already made. Yet their not-yet-made weapon is monstrous, monstrous enough to warrant international or national force, whereas our thousands of weapons do not seem to make us criminal in our own minds. We can say that this is in part because we trust that these would never be used. But we have to then say, "What if we were living someplace else where we were potentially on the receiving end rather than giving end? Would it look like they couldn't be used? Why did those seventy-eight countries in 1995 go to the International Court of Justice and ask that they be declared illegal?" Something that is often forgotten is that, in the 1990s, we gained in our major strategic nuclear arsenal. The heart of our nuclear arsenal is Ohio-class submarines. We have 18 of them. Each of them carries the equivalent of four thousand Hiroshima bombs. After the opening of the Berlin Wall in 1989–90, we acquired 8 of those 18 Ohio-class submarines. So, thirty-two thousand Hiroshima-size bombs were acquired by our country during the 1990s. It is an incredible act of nonsymmetrical thinking not to recognize what this looks like to other countries, and especially those that are signers of the nonproliferation treaty. But your question goes beyond the example of nuclear weapons.

Some mental exercises that are advocated by philosophers, like Bertrand Russell's rotation of nouns, are useful. If you take any sentence that you see in the newspaper that describes what

the United States is doing, what Iraq is doing, what Egypt is
doing, what Britain is doing, and scramble the names and nouns
and see where the moral balance of the sentence lies once you
change the position of the names, it is a very useful exercise.
There may be some reasons why that exercise is not *always* valid,
but it is at least a good way of keeping one's mind limber so that
you know you are judging the quality of the act and not simply
reexperiencing the stuck position of the nouns and subjects and
objects in the sentence.

It is also the case that one can read a great deal more about
these countries, which I think all of us are doing. It is important
to read across a political spectrum of views. In my own case, I
have learned a great deal by reading Ken Pollack's book *The
Threatening Storm,* which is an argument for why we should
invade Iraq. I do not believe for a minute that we should invade
Iraq. Yet the book has a lot of important information in it. Also,
one should know what the best arguments are on the other side.
That means if some of you are on the side for invading Iraq, then
it is important to read the best arguments that are available
on the side of not invading Iraq. At a poetry reading two weeks
ago held at the American Repertory Theatre, many of the poems
were written by either American or British poets, but a number
of the poems were by authors from either Iraq or Iran or other
countries in that region. It actually did give a kind of perspective
that is not there if you do not have the lyrical utterances of the
other people and you only hear your own thoughts in a range of
vocabularies that goes from high moral argument to lyric utter-
ance. The other side is essentially underrepresented in any lin-
guistic mode other than the most narrow.

Question: We have seen a frightening capacity for abuse in the name of security that has come at the official level in the wake of 9-11. If the larger portion of the population were emboldened by a feeling of personal responsibility for the safety of others, what would prevent these untrained individuals from acting in ways that would be more discriminatory, reactionary, and even less accountable to public justice than the current system of security from an official level?

ES: At first you were asking about the U.S. Patriot Act and the abridgments of privacy that have come from our own government that requires libraries to turn over lists of what books people read. We know that by early this year, according to a University of Illinois study, 5 percent of all libraries have had requests made of them and 11 percent of all libraries in towns of populations of fifty thousand or more. We know that by February of 2002, two hundred university registrars had been asked for information about students. In some cases the request for information may be legitimate. If a foreign person claims to be a student at a school, there should be verification that the person really is a student at the school. But certain other kinds of information are not legitimate points of inquiry.

Now your worry is not that such government practices are invasive but that if we begin to watch each other, we will be invasive. I do not think that we should begin to watch each other in the way that Bush's TIPS program imagined. I think that we have become infantilized as a population and all the important tasks of defending the country have been taken out of our hands so that we are expected just to turn on the TV and see what is being done in the name of our country. When we are in this infantilized position, we cannot remember what it is people did when they were in the mature position in charge of their country. They did not normally perform acts of vigilantism on each other; they did not normally take the occasion to turn each other in. Yes, there are instances of such acts, but this country survived for a long time with a population where people watched out for themselves and their communities as a whole. I do not think we should be bullied into thinking that either our patriarchs have to watch out for us or, if we do it, we are going to start turning into them and abridging one another's privacy.

Question: In your article on nuclear double standard, you say that nuclear weapons are inhumane and imply that we should disarm. What would you say to the argument that while the creation of nuclear weapons was obviously not a good thing, now that they do exist, the only way to actually prevent nuclear war is to maintain a huge deterrent? While it may be immoral to keep millions of others living under the threat of genocide, and while this may perpetuate asymmetrical notions of otherness, in practice, the threat of mutually assured destruction is the only thing that kept the cold war from going nuclear and that maintains baseline geopolitical stability today.

ES: I would say that that is a completely wrong argument. Nonetheless, it is an argument that more than one smart person has made, so it is perfectly fine that you should raise the issue. But it is absolutely wrong. We can look now at that 1995 International Court of Justice case. Among the many countries that came there asking for a judgment of illegality were India and North Korea, two countries that did not then have nuclear weapons. Is it any surprise that they decided that if the United States and other powers were going to stand there and argue that such weapons are compatible with international law—that using nuclear weapons would not constitute an act of genocide, would

not be incompatible with human rights covenants, would not
abridge environmental treaties—is it any wonder that India and
North Korea went on to get nuclear weapons? The idea that by
having them we deter does not make sense. In an article in *The
Nation,* Jonathan Schell makes the argument, "Actually the deterrence theory is a pro-proliferation theory." He does not just
pull that sentence out of a hat. He goes through a careful set of
steps showing how this thing just keeps mushrooming. The
other book that I would urge you to read is Paul Bracken's *Fire
in the East: The Rise of Asian Military Power and the Second
Nuclear Age* (about India, Pakistan, North Korea, China, etc.).
Bracken is someone who, during the cold war, had very important books on command and control of nuclear weapons.
Bracken says, "Look. We never left the first nuclear age. Even
though nobody in the United States wanted to talk about it, we
never left it. But whether we left it or not, we are now in the second nuclear age because now we are in a situation where lots of
countries are getting it, countries that do not necessarily have
the brakes on using it."

The only chance for pulling back from proliferation and asking the whole world to give up nuclear weapons and other
weapons of mass destruction is for the United States to take a
lead. The United States will only take a lead in it if the population asks for our country to do so. It is interesting to me that we
seldom say to our leaders, "By the way, when you were in office,
did you ever contemplate using nuclear weapons?" Any president who has been asked that question has said yes, he has contemplated using them. Yet we normally do not even think that
that is a question we need to ask, nor do we think we should look
at the kind of presidential deliberation that took place during his

office. If we did look closely at it, we would feel much less comfortable about calmly saying we never get very close. I looked, for example, at two sets of presidential papers. As you may know, when Congress argues something, the debate is public, something you can watch; in usual cases where it takes place in a closed session, it is immediately published after the deliberations are over. Presidential papers are not that way. Usually thirty, fifty years elapse before the record of deliberation becomes available. But I looked at some from recently released papers fifty years ago, namely in the Eisenhower administration. Eisenhower contemplated using nuclear weapons in the 1954 Taiwan Straits crisis and again in 1959 in Berlin. If we had in front of us the presidential papers for subsequent administrations, we would also find that they have, as various presidents have acknowledged, contemplated using nuclear weapons at different times.

Question: In not supporting the International Court, the U.S. seems to feel it does not need to follow the same rules as other countries as the world's major superpower. Is there anything U.S. citizens or other countries can do about this elitism?

ES: Yes. This year there have been a number of good articles about American elitism or American exceptionalism and the danger of coming to think that you do not have to play by the shared rules. We know that other countries and individual people living elsewhere in the world think that the United States needs to play by the rules.

Now your specific question: Is there anything that the American people can do about it? What we can do about it is know what the laws are and insist that they be followed. There are two sets of rules. One is our own constitutional, national laws. The others are the ones you referred to: the international laws. We need to play by both sets of rules. Some of you are going to go on and become journalists or teachers or enter some other job where you might have the chance to make sure that when there is an international principle or a national principle that is being violated you will be able to write about it. One striking thing about that world court case was that it was almost never spoken about in any newspaper in this country. Other countries were covering it. Despite the fact that it was going on for weeks and months, it was not considered newsworthy here. Part of the reason for that is that it presented a damaging view of us, but it is to our advantage to understand what the damaging view is. If it is a wrong view, we can outargue it; but if we do not know what it is, we actually put ourselves at risk.

In this attempt to know the laws and make sure that the laws themselves are widely known, and to make sure that we live by them, I think that people often tend to favor the international over the national, so I will just take a minute to say that the national laws are also crucial. In fact, if there is only one set of laws that you are going to follow, the most important to follow are the national. When you watch a vote of the UN, how many people are voting on a certain issue? The UN is crucial, as are our international laws. But the number of people who are voting is tiny compared to the number of people that are represented in national votes. That is why we can be in this situation where the leaders of certain countries are pledging their country's support of us, and the populations are 80 percent against. Because the leaders alone constitute a small international group.

Since I work on human rights, I sometimes have the great pleasure of being in international meetings with people from

other countries who work on international rights. There will often come a point in the conversation where people will say, "Do
not use national laws to uphold this right. Use international ones
because national ones are so local and parochial." Well, what is
the international community at that point? I am in a room with
20 people, and we are 20 people and we feel transnational because one person is from Ethiopia and one person is from the
United States and one person is from France. But we are just 20
people, whereas when you have the internal laws of Ethiopia and
the internal laws of France and the internal laws of the United
States, you have a huge population of people that have borne
witness to those laws and have pledged to stand by them. Both
international laws and national laws should be followed, but in
this era ahead, one should not be hoodwinked into thinking that
it is somehow more high-minded and cosmopolitan to turn your
back on anything that sounds like it is national and only follow
international rules.

Question: You mentioned earlier the infantilization of the American
voting public. I was hoping you might expand a little bit on that
concept.

ES: It is important to know that one's full stature in the civilian realm
has tended to follow from having a full stature in the military
realm; that is, for taking responsibility for military decisions. I
will give you three important examples. The Fifteenth Amendment, which extended the right to vote to African Americans,
was argued primarily on the basis that 180,000 blacks had fought
in the Civil War and therefore it was inconceivable that they
should not be included in the voting population. Later on, the
Nineteenth Amendment, which extended the right to vote to
women, was similarly argued on the basis that women had the

capacity to defend themselves and that their contributions to the defense of the country were important in World War I; the same arguments, yoking suffrage and women's military stature, were made in other countries such as Britain and Russia. Most recently, the Twenty-sixth Amendment, which lowered the voting age from 21 to 18, was argued primarily on the basis of Vietnam: old enough to fight, old enough to vote. A twin argument was put forward in the congressional deliberations. One was that people had fought in Vietnam at 18; the other was that people had deliberated about Vietnam on university campuses. Members of Congress and other witnesses of the Vietnam generation said that this was the most politically responsible generation the country had seen. People from all sides of the political spectrum said that. They even had anthropologist Margaret Mead testify that the original voting age of 21 had come from the fact that people in the past only had strong enough bone structures to carry their armor once they were 21. But now, due to good nutrition, people can carry their armor at 18.

Now you can see that in each of those three areas one's civil stature depends in part on bearing military responsibility. We often hear today from the gay community that by being discriminated against militarily, their civil stature is jeopardized as well. That claim is accurate. What is not often enough said is that it is not just people who are gay who are discriminated against; it is all of us. Because from no one's intention but through a kind of accident of technology we have come to have monarchic weapons that require only a small number of people to fire them, and therefore we have forms of military authorization that also require small numbers of people.

There is one important postscript I should add, because I

know that it is alarming to people when I say that we should bear military responsibility. The right to bear arms is a distributive right, as many of the first ten amendments are in the Bill of Rights. The right to bear arms is saying that however much injuring power the country has, the say over it, the authorization over it, has to be distributed to the whole country. That question is prior to any question about whether we will have a lot of injuring power or none at all. The fact that I say this decision-making power about whether the country goes to war is really something that the whole population is responsible for, does not mean we are going to have the whole population carrying arms. To illustrate this, I will use the example of the fact that both militarists and pacifists have saluted the right to bear arms. Mirabeau in the French Revolution said that revolution was needed because the aristocracy had deprived the whole population of their arms. More surprising is the fact that Gandhi once said of all the evil acts committed by the British against India, the worst is the disarming of the population. Give us back our arms, and then we will tell you whether or not we are going to use them. Gandhi's decision, as I am sure you know, was that we should not use arms. But he was making the point that you are not even in a position to dissent, are not even in a position to urge nonviolence, unless you are in a position to contribute to the military decisions that your country is making.

Question: You have been involved in helping Ethiopia formulate its constitution. If a newly established state were having a convention to plan its constitution, and the people involved wanted you to come and offer some insights from "The Difficulty of Imagining Other Persons," what questions would you encourage them to think about as they were planning the legal basis for a society?

ES: Here I am lucky because I have the American Constitution in front of my eyes. Tom Paine once said, "The American Constitution is to liberty what an alphabet is to language." It is something that shows us the parts that need to be there, even though there are now many other constitutions that also help us to get this vision. Key in the making of the U.S. Constitution were the war-making provisions. Justice Story, in the nineteenth century, said that Article 1, Section 8, Clause 11 of the Constitution, which requires a congressional declaration, is the cornerstone of the whole Constitution. I would see the right to bear arms as on that same level of fundamental importance.

The second thing I would say is something that the ratifiers said when the Constitution of the United States was going out to the states for ratification: You may not realize that the Bill of Rights—the first ten amendments that are so precious to us that give freedom of speech, freedom of assembly, freedom of religion, right against cruel and unusual punishment, right against search and seizure—those things were not in the Constitution until it went out to the ratification assemblies. The ratification assemblies said, "Wait. We are not signing this unless it makes explicit what the rights are." Finally, it was the state of New York that made it clear that they were not going to go ahead unless these guarantees were made explicit and put in the Constitution. I would say to any new constitution makers, "Do not assume that it goes without saying that you have whatever rights are not in there." It has got to be said what the rights are. As Patrick Henry said during the ratification debates, "What good is it going to do me to say it is an implied right to be free of cruelty when I am in the midst of being subjected to cruel and unusual punishment?"

NOAM CHOMSKY, linguist

Noam Chomsky is professor of linguistics and philosophy at the Massachusetts Institute of Technology. Beginning in the 1950s, Chomsky revolutionized his academic field by demonstrating that languages share a universal grammar based on innate structures of the human mind. Although his professional area of study is linguistics, Chomsky's presence is just as substantive in the political realm. A leading figure in the global justice movement, Chomsky scrutinizes state power and the propaganda system on which it relies. Among his more than one hundred books are Hegemony or Survival: America's Quest for Global Dominance, 9-11, *and* Manufacturing Consent: The Political Economy of the Mass Media *(with Edward S. Herman). In this interview, Chomsky discusses the origins of his social engagement, the systematic biases of foreign affairs coverage, the recruitment of children into consumerism, and his own sources of hope.*

Question: In the *Guardian* article "Conscience of a Nation," Maya Jaggi reports that during your childhood you felt there was no one to talk to. When Hiroshima was bombed, you found it shocking that nobody seemed to care. I wonder how you dealt with having no one to talk to. What were your initial reactions and thoughts when you discovered no one cared? How were you able to become such a staunch defender of the losing side?

Noam Chomsky: When you are a child, you do not really think about things much. You just take the world the way it is. On a lot of issues nobody cared. But I don't want to exaggerate. I grew up in the 1930s, and it was a very lively period. The people in my family were first-generation immigrants, and a lot of them were unemployed: working-class seamstresses and shop boys. Many of them were involved in a lively range of active politics of that period, so it was not as if nobody cared. The incident you mentioned happened to be at a summer camp. The atom bombs were in August, and I was a junior counselor at this summer camp. There was not much news. We had camped and heard a radio report. It was obvious that something horrendous had happened and striking that nobody seemed to notice. I went off by myself to the woods for a couple of hours, and when I came back still nobody noticed.

The same thing happens now. In these respects, very little changes. We do not notice when we do things to other people. When they do something to us, we notice. But when we do it to them, it just did not happen. That is true of the most educated, liberal, sophisticated circles like, say, Harvard.

You probably read the *New York Times* and the Sunday *Times Book Review*, and I wonder how many noticed the week before last that there was a book review in the *New York Times Book Review* by a very good, very distinguished, and very fine American historian. There was a book about early American history, which the author of the review said brought out the negative side of U.S. history, namely that there are people who cheat and run scams and so on. In passing, in a kind of throwaway line, he mentioned that in the course of the conquest of the national territory, hundreds of thousands of indigenous people were eliminated. It was not hundreds of thousands—it was many millions. And they were not just eliminated. If you read the founding fathers, you will see that they were well aware that, as John Quincy Adams put it, they were "exterminating the hapless race of Native

Americans." Does anybody notice? Suppose you read in the German press today that during the Second World War, several hundred thousand Jews were eliminated. We would notice that. In fact, we might say it was a return of Nazism, and we better nuke them or something. But this one does not count because we did it. After all, they were just the "merciless Indian savages" whom King George III unleashed against us, one of his many crimes listed in the Declaration of Independence. They were the Indians whom my friends and I used to shoot in the woods when we were eight years old playing cowboys and Indians.

Today, there was a news report of an Apache helicopter shot down over Fallujah. Can you think of any other country that names its most merciless offensive weapons after victims of genocide? It is inconceivable, but we do it.

It is better now than it was thirty or forty years ago. Thirty or forty years ago, comments like the one I mentioned from the *New York Times*—that was mainstream history. If you studied anthropology back in the 1960s, you learned that there were maybe a million hunter-gatherers wandering around somewhere who did not really own anything—that was proven by John Locke—so the land was basically open and they simply took it. You can read a standard diplomatic history of the U.S. written again by a very good liberal historian, Thomas Bailey, in 1969, which discusses the Revolution and says that after the Revolution, the colonists turned to their next task, which was "felling trees and Indians and rounding out their natural boundaries." That would not be tolerable anymore. There are a lot of changes, but there is a long way to go.

Question: Do you believe that universities can be nonpolitical? On a more personal level, how have you yourself negotiated between being faithful to your beliefs and accepting socialization in order to gain the authority you now have as university professor and renowned political thinker?

NC: When I went to Harvard, this university did not look like this. It was well-dressed white males. I went through not only Harvard but the ultrasocialization sector of Harvard, the Harvard Society of Fellows, where you were socialized into the ways of the elite—how to dress, how to act, how to talk. No women, of course, in those days, except for the women who served the elegant meals. You can survive it. You have a choice; you do not have to conform to it. Plenty of people did not conform to it; that is why Harvard looks the way it does today. The country was civilized by the activism of the 1960s. That is why the sixties are so hated, and if you take a course about the sixties, they will probably tell you how awful it was. It was awful: it democratized the country; it civilized the country; it raised all kinds of issues that were off the agenda like women's rights, civil rights, and the environment (a lot of things you were not supposed to think about, and did not think about). It is different now, but similar pressures exist. They exist all the way up through the educational system and the political system.

For example, we are having something in November called an election. Suppose someone from Mars was watching this and trying to figure out what was going on. There are two candidates, both of them born to great wealth and political power. Both of them went to the same elite university; both of them joined the same secret society where they were socialized into the manners and style of the ruling class; and both of them are able to run because they are supported by basically the same narrow concentrations of economic power. Is that an election?

By some standards it is. By others, it would be considered a failed state. But we accept it because we are indoctrinated into accepting it. Unless you do some research, you won't find out that this is by no means universal.

Another example is Haiti. Haiti is the poorest country in the hemisphere; the United States is the richest country in the hemisphere. Haiti is what we call a failed state. The recent period that led to Haiti being a failed state starts in 1990, when Haiti had its first free election after an awful history. It was taken for granted that the victor in the election would be the U.S. candidate. No one had been paying attention, but in Haiti a real democratic society had developed of the kind we cannot even imagine. There had been a lot of organizing and activism in the slums and in the hills, where almost all the population lives in extreme poverty. When it got to the point where a lively civil society had developed, they were able to elect their own candidate—a populist priest named Aristide who came to office in 1991. In the richest country in the hemisphere, that is an unimaginable election; in the poorest country in the hemisphere, they could carry it off. It is interesting to notice what happened and how Haiti descended into becoming a more desperate place than it was.

The U.S. was utterly appalled by the election and immediately withdrew its funding to the government and instead diverted the funding to what is called the democratic opposition, which is a technical term that means business groups and other groups that want to subordinate the country to the U.S. The U.S. was so appalled by the election that it actually changed its immigration policies. As for judgment of Harvard, that is for you to make. You are here, so you decide if it is free, open, critical, and

adversarial. In your history courses, for example, were there bit-
ter condemnations of the horrendous comment I just quoted or
not? You can decide.

The U.S. had an immigration policy towards Haiti; it was
completely illegal and radically in violation of elementary principles of international humanitarian law and the Universal Declaration of Human Rights. The U.S. had Haiti under a blockade
that was instituted by President Carter, part of elevating human
rights to be the soul of our foreign policy. Haiti was then under
the rule of brutal, murderous dictators supported by the U.S.,
which meant that anyone fleeing Haiti was by definition an
economic refugee, not a political refugee, and therefore they
were not allowed out of the country. If they made it here,
they were sent back. You are not a political refugee if you escape
the torture chamber of a dictator that we are supporting. That
changed when they had democratic elections. For the first time,
the U.S. began accepting refugees as political refugees because
they were fleeing from a country that had a democratically
elected president. It did not really matter much because not a
lot of people were fleeing the country. In fact, the flow was in the
other direction. It was a moment of hope. But the official policy
was shifted.

Well, policy went back to normal in September 1991, when
the anticipated military coup took place and a murderous, brutal gang of thugs took power—a military junta supported by
a tiny rich elite. Then U.S. policy went back to the norm; from
then on people fleeing became economic refugees again and
they could not get in. The Organization of the American States
imposed an embargo on Haiti. George Bush the first announced
right away that the United States was going to violate it; that is,
he exempted U.S. firms from the embargo. The *New York Times*

described it as a humanitarian move of what they called fine-tuning the embargo for the benefit of the people of Haiti. In fact, the U.S. trade with Haiti, meaning the junta and the rich elite, continued while the population was being ground in the dust. I was there during the period of the terror, and it was really horrendous. It turned out later that under Clinton trade increased. It also turned out, though it has yet to be reported outside the business press, that the Clinton administration had authorized the Texaco oil company to ship oil to the military junta in violation of presidential directives. Think about it for a moment: oil is the core part of an embargo. The CIA was reporting regularly to Congress that all flow of oil to Haiti had been stopped. Meanwhile, if you walked around the streets of Port-au-Prince, you could see the oil farms being built by the rich families and the oil tankers in the harbor.

Finally, in September 1994, the Clinton administration decided that the population had been tortured enough and they permitted the elected president to return. There is a phrase for that here—it is called restoring democracy—and we are very proud of it because it shows our commitment to democracy. But what no one bothers to report is that Clinton permitted Aristide to return, but on the condition that he accept the program of the defeated U.S. candidate in the 1990 election. You can return, you can have democracy, as long as you do what we tell you and not what the people in the slums and hills voted for. That is what we call restoring democracy. (According to what Mr. Summers told you, you all know all this because it is very important news, right on the front pages, recent history, and, of course, in a free university everybody would know about it. But let's continue anyway.)

The program that the Clinton administration imposed on the

government as it returned was a very harsh neoliberal program
of a kind which Mr. Summers administered in his former life in
the Treasury Department, a program which opened Haiti's
economy completely to a flow of foreign goods. What does that
mean? For example, Haitian rice farmers are very poor, but they
are pretty efficient. However, they cannot conceivably compete
with exports from U.S. agribusiness, which gets maybe 40 percent of its profits from subsidies that are given to them by the
Reagan administration in accord with our love of free market.
Naturally, as was predicted, Haitian rice farmers were wiped
out. Now we lament that Haiti somehow cannot feed itself. Big
surprise. It is the miracle of the market. Haiti did have a couple
of small industries that were working. For example, the industry
of packaging chicken parts was functioning and making some
money. It turns out that Americans do not like dark meat, so the
big corporations like Tyson have a lot of extra dark meet on their
hands, and they would like to dump it somewhere. They tried to
dump it on Canada and Mexico, but they did not have democracy restored there, so they were able to impose antidumping restrictions. However, Haiti is different; there, thanks to our love
of democracy, they cannot stop it. Therefore, chicken parts were
dumped on Haiti, and that killed that industry.

It was perfectly obvious in 1994 that the program the U.S. was
forcing on Haiti was going to destroy what was left of the economy and drive the country into chaos and disruption. That is
what happened. It imploded pretty predictably. Bush the second
made it worse by blocking foreign aid on completely frivolous
grounds, but by then the damage had already been done. If you
look at the reporting in the last few weeks, it is all about Haiti,
the failed state, where we tried to do nation building because we

are so magnificent, and we tried to restore democracy. But they
have a bad culture or maybe bad genes or something, so they just
could not handle it and fell apart. Maybe we should go back and
try nation building even harder since we worked so well at it the
first time. Well, that's Haiti. Who is the failed state again? Is it
the state that actually had a democratic election of extremely
poor people over terrible odds and managed to elect their own
candidate? Or is it the state that crushed it and would not toler-
ate that and is having an election of the kind we are having in
November?

Again, in a free and independent critical university, these
questions would be the obvious ones; maybe so obvious that you
would not even bother talking about them because the answers
are so clear. But you can judge how prominent they are in the
curriculum here and in the discussions and then make your own
evaluation. There are plenty of other cases. I will just mention
one. There was an election in Spain a couple of weeks ago. The
Spanish people committed a major crime: they voted out a government that had gone to war over the opposition of 90 percent
of the population but following orders from Crawford, Texas, so
it was considered the right thing to do. They were the good guys.
New Europe they were called. Okay, they were voted out. How
many of you saw a report saying that the Spanish people were
voting for a position held by about 70 percent of Americans?
About 70 percent of Americans believe that security, political
transfer, and economic development in Iraq should be in the
hands of the United Nations with the U.S. playing a role as part
of a multilateral system. That is what Spain voted for. They did
not vote to pull the troops out. They voted to not allow troops in
unless it was under UN authorization, approximately the posi-

tion of 70 percent of the American public. Well, what is the difference between Spain and the United States? One difference is that in Spain everybody knows what public opinion is.

In the United States, nobody knows what public opinion is. You can find out the information I just told you by going to the major polling institutions in the United States like the Program on International Policy Attitudes at University of Maryland, which does in-depth public opinion studies, the most sophisticated in the world. You can look them up on the Internet, and you will find out what I just told you. The people who have those views presumably think they are the only ones in the world who believe that way; they certainly do not see it articulated anywhere, reported, or discussed. Another difference is that in Spain, as distinct from here, issues that people are concerned about come up in elections. This issue is not going to come up in the U.S. election; it came up in the Spanish election, and people could vote the way they felt. Which is the failed state? It would be easy to go on. These ought to be truisms in my opinion; they ought to be things you really would not study at Harvard because you would know them already. But if you do not study them and you do not study them at Harvard, there is a problem somewhere.

Question: How does your research on the negative effects the media can have affect your views on the way that we should raise our children?

NC: First of all, if you are well educated, you should not be using the word "children." There is a technical term for those small things: they are called "evolving consumers." I am not joking. In the institution that pretty much runs the country—the public relations industry that serves the business world, which spends maybe two trillion dollars on marketing, maybe a sixth of the GDP (it runs elections, and it is the core of the media and information systems)—they have some principles. One of the principles is to keep the population passive and obedient and marginalized. It was recognized in the 1920s in the more free countries, like England and the United States, that people have won too much freedom for it to be possible to control them simply by force the way it had been done in the past. Therefore, you had to control their attitudes and opinions and beliefs—more subtle ways of controlling them. That is when the public relations industry and the advertising business took off. It was frankly called propaganda in those days. The leading figure in the industry wrote a major textbook called *Propaganda,* which was about how to control people's minds and attitudes to make sure that the enlightened minority, namely us, can run the place without being bothered by the rabble. The rabble will be off doing their own things. They have to be directed to what were called the superficial things of life, like fashionable consumption, and you have to impose on them a philosophy of futility, a sense that they really can't do anything, and so they might as well buy shoes. Then you have to control their beliefs too, so that they do not see things like the kinds of things I was just talking about in, say, Haiti.

It is rather striking that this industry developed in the free countries, in England and the United States, and there is a good reason for that. This was the period of development in industry of what is called Taylorism, which is an industrial system designed to turn workers into robots, to control every motion precisely, so that workers would have no independence or creativity or initiative on the job. It was called on-job control. That was a

really exciting development; it was picked up all over. Lenin, for
example, was extremely enthusiastic about it, and they introduced it right away after the Bolshevik Revolution. It was, inci-
dentally, developed in the military industry in the U.S. But that's
normal. Contrary to what you are taught in economics courses,
we do not have a free-enterprise, free-market economy. We have
an economy based extensively on the dynamic state sector of the
economy; that is where almost all of what is called the new economy comes from. If anything comes out of it, you hand it over to
Bill Gates or someone, and you privatize profits. You can run
through the leading elements of the economy and check it out;
it goes way back. So Taylorism was developed in the military industry, where it is cost free and risk free because it is socialized,
but when it worked out, it was transferred over to private industry. It did not take long for people to realize that if we can have
on-job control with people, we ought to be able to have off-job
control. Why should they be uncontrolled in the rest of their
lives? How do we carry off off-job control? By propaganda, as it
was frankly called then. Advertising, induced consumerism, imposed passivity, marginalization. That is the core of a lot of the
raising of so-called children; let's come back to the "evolving
consumer."

In recent decades, the public relations industry has recognized that there is a class of people who are being underutilized
in the system; they are there, but they do not have any money.
How do you get them to buy and to become consumers, which is
what they are supposed to be? They don't have any money, so
they can't buy, but they can get their parents to buy. How do children get their parents to buy? Maybe you still remember: the
way you do it is by nagging your parents. There is now a field of

academic applied psychology that is literally the study of nagging; it turns out that there are half a dozen different ways of
nagging, and different kinds have to be stimulated for different
kinds of purchases. If you can get the kids to nag their parents
enough, then maybe the parents will buy the eight-hundred-
dollar mechanical dog or something, which the kid will throw
away in five minutes or so because it is too boring. If you think
that is an exaggeration, you are wrong. I have grandchildren and
I can see it happening. That is a way of getting off-job control
down to infancy. If you watch television programs for infants,
you will notice that they are drenched in it.

One of the glories of the American economy in the last twenty
years in what is called the neoliberal period outside the U.S.—
in the U.S. there is not a name for it; it is better not to talk about
it, so we don't have a word for it—is that there has been some
economic growth, but it is narrowly concentrated. For example,
if you look at real wages in the last two decades, real wages have
stagnated or declined for a large majority of the population.
For—I think it is—.01 percent of the population it has increased
by 600 percent. People are getting by, but you can't find another
period of economic history, except during wars and famines and
so on, where there has been such long stagnation for most of the
population. Furthermore, work hours have sharply increased.
Back in 1980, American workers were at the low end of the industrial world; now they are way at the top, long ago passing
Japan and other industrial countries. Now two parents have to
work to keep things going, particularly when you are under
tremendous pressure for mass consumption. You are supposed
to "max out" five credit cards, and you have kids nagging for
things, and your income is barely stable. Furthermore, benefits

are declining. The tax burden has sharply shifted during the neoliberal period, so the percentage of tax paid by corporations has sharply declined, and the percentage of taxes that comes from the very regressive taxes, like payroll taxes have gone way up, which shifts the burden to the poor. That means that for most of the population, they are working very hard just to keep going; there is little in the way of sensible day care, they do not have much in the way of benefits, they are in debt; they are worried about their futures; the kids are nagging. How are you going to raise your kids? Well, you can subject them to the huge propaganda system that is turning them into evolving consumers.

Meanwhile, the public schools are underfunded on purpose. If you want to destroy a public school system, what you do is underfund it so that it doesn't work. Then you say the only answer is privatization, so you hand it over to unaccountable private tyrannies called corporations. They make it even worse, but then what can you do? The British railway system is a perfect example; our health system is a good example. You underfund the schools, people want out, and you work out various devices, like vouchers. Sooner or later, if they get bad enough, people will not want them anymore, and then you will have eliminated that source of democratization and egalitarian development.

So what do you do about raising your children? You teach them how to protect themselves from this hurricane. You can do it. In fact, one of the reasons that the country has become so much better in the last twenty to thirty years is that a lot of people did protect themselves from it. It is not irresistible.

Question: Who or what has inspired you now and in the past? What keeps you from becoming too disillusioned?

NC: The second question is the easiest. Just think about the world forty years ago and the world today. There's quite a significant change across the board—attitudes, beliefs, personal behaviors, interactions, the way you dress. Think back to the sixties and what there wasn't. There wasn't a women's movement. There wasn't an environmental movement. There was virtually no antiwar movement. That came in the late sixties, after years and years of war. There was no Third World solidarity movement, no global justice movement. All sorts of things that are part of our lives just didn't exist.

These changes have come over the last forty years because people aren't willing to become disillusioned. Either you can say "I give up," in which case you can be sure the worst is going to happen, or you can say "Okay, I'm going to be committed to trying to make things better" and make things better. So there's nothing to be disillusioned about.

As to what's inspiring, it's the way people struggle. You see it all over the world. I recently went to both Turkey (including Kurdish areas) and Colombia, two countries that are very high on the list of violence and atrocities and also happen to be, not by accident, the two leading recipients of U.S. military aid, aside from Israel and Egypt, which are a separate category. The U.S. under Clinton provided 80 percent of the arms for atrocities in Turkey. In fact, in a single year in 1997, Clinton sent more arms to Turkey than during the entire cold war period up to the onset of the state terror campaign against the Kurds in the early 1990s. It's not a small thing. Turkey was replaced in the lead by Colombia in 1999 because it had succeeded in crushing its own Kurdish population, and Colombia had not yet succeeded in its own terrorist activities, so it went to the top. Now the U.S. press is finally sometimes reporting these stories about Turkey because

the Turkish government did not succumb to Washington's demands and coercion. As a punishment, impassioned articles by
liberal people are published about the rotten things the Turkish
government did in the 1990s. All true, but they are not reporting that we provided the arms and military training for that purpose and that they kept quiet about it so that it could not be
stopped by popular opposition. These are little items worth
knowing if you're an American citizen.

The people are not giving up. Turkish and Colombian intel-
lectuals don't ask, "What can I do?" Writers, journalists, artists,
and academic figures are constantly carrying out protests. In
Colombia, they get their heads blown off. In Turkey, they can get
sent to Turkish prisons for years or much of their lives for telling
what's going on. They're not giving up, just like campesinos and
indigenous peoples and Afro-Colombians who are being driven
off their lands by chemical warfare and fumigation with U.S. aid
and U.S. military forces.

But they're not complaining; they're constantly protesting.

Question: Suppose that the media are business propaganda. If we
can't trust the media or our leaders, who can we trust? And
where can we get real information?

NC: On the media being business propaganda, again that is not very
original. It is one of the same things that George Orwell pointed
out in his introduction to *Animal Farm*. One of the reasons he
gave for the conformism in the British media (his phrase): "The
press is owned by wealthy men who have every reason not to
want certain ideas to be expressed." That is pretty brief, and you
have to go on. But if you go on, the institutional framework in
which the media function has an effect of restricting what comes
out. This is also true of government media. NPR is supposed to

be on the critical side but very narrowly, not a millimeter off a certain line, and basic assumptions are accepted.

Who should you trust? Same as if you were taking a chemistry course: nobody. If you go over to the science department, they don't teach you to trust people. You are not supposed to trust the teacher or the book or anything else. If you are studying to be a scientist, you are trained to trust your own mind. You investigate. Of course, you pay attention to what people say. You do not say, "I think the theory of relativity is wrong," but you are not supposed to accept what you are taught as God given. In fact, if you are a good scientist, you are going to challenge it all the time. That is what experiments are for. That is what doctoral dissertations are for. Most of them challenge things; otherwise they are not very interesting. Do it on the basis of your own intelligence, and your own critical faculties, and your own understanding. You do not automatically say everything is rot, but you do approach things with a skeptical attitude. That is the whole point. Why should it be any different in the much more important domain of human affairs?

You have got to approach things with critical, skeptical attitudes, particularly in the domain of human affairs even more than in science. Mother Nature is not trying to make things easy for you, but she is not trying to lie to you, either, and control you and shape your attitudes. In the other domains, that is exactly what is happening, so you have to be even more skeptical, quite apart from the fact that understanding is much more shallow, so it does not take that much to figure out what is going on. There are no deep theories around, so you don't trust anyone except your own critical intelligence.

2. LABOR AND ECONOMY
Working It Out

ROBERT REICH, political scholar

As Bill Clinton's secretary of labor, Robert Reich helped to pass the Family and Medical Leave Act, leading a national fight against sweatshops and heading the campaign that raised the minimum wage. Under his leadership, the Department of Labor earned more than thirty awards for innovation and government reinvention. Reich resigned from his cabinet post in order to spend more time with his family. Since then, Reich has worked as a cofounder and national editor of The American Prospect *magazine, a 2002 Massachusetts gubernatorial candidate, and a professor of social and economic policy at Brandeis University. In 2003 he won the Václav Havel Prize, awarded annually to a person whose work has significantly addressed fundamental problems of humanity. He is the author of ten books, including, most recently,* Reason: Why Liberals Will Win the Battle for America. *In this interview, Reich discusses the ethics and economics of the global marketplace and grassroots politics, never losing sight of the common good.*

Robert Reich: I should say that I approach this class with some trepidation because in the sister course we were talking about politics, personal choice, personal efficacy, and the ability to feel that you can actually have an effect on your society. Somehow during the course of that session, I got into my head that I should run for the governor of Massachusetts. And I lost. So just be careful what you say. Anything could happen in this session. Let me urge every one of you to at some point in your life—you do not have to run for governor—to take electoral politics very seriously. If, because of cynicism or resignation, you decide that politics is somebody else's business, you are ceding the political arena to the other guys. I have said this before: politics is the applied form of democracy. Unless we understand it and practice it and take it seriously and really be part of the political process, we are not effectively utilizing our power in this democracy and we are not experiencing what this democracy is really about. End of commercial. Your question.

Question: Everyone knows people in the workplace who have been downsized, fired, restructured, or simply quit of their own accord. It seems that loyalty in the American workplace is dead. In your opinion, what has led to this death in company employee loyalty? How do globalization and new technologies in the workplace figure into this?

RR: If you roll the tape back thirty years ago, when I was in college, the assumption was that most of us graduates could get jobs if we wanted to. Very few of us wanted this, but you could get a job in a company, stay at the company for twenty, thirty, or forty years, retire with a little gold chain, a little watch, and a good pension. You would get a good salary. If you happened to be an hourly worker—and most people who went to college were not destined to be hourly workers, but most people did not go to college, and therefore, most people were hourly workers—if you were an hourly worker, you would not be laid off, except in times of recession. But the term "layoff" itself implied that you would get back "on" when the recession was over. You would have unemployment insurance during the recession, and you would get your job back. Now, was that a system of loyalty? Using the term "loyalty" implies that there was some special sentiment of collective, shared fate between a company and its employees. I think it is a little bit more complicated than that.

Thirty years ago, most of the leading industries in America—auto, steel, manufacturing, and even insurance industries—were organized as oligopolies. Three, four, or five major players roughly coordinated their investments and their outputs. The key to success was economies of scale—more runs, longer and longer runs of more product. If you could produce more, you could amortize your fixed costs over many, many units and therefore generate profits. Thirty years ago, labor unions were fairly powerful. In fact, go back a little further; in 1955 roughly 35 percent of American workers were unionized, and most of those unionized workers set prevailing wages in their industries. If only four or five major manufacturers or players are in an industry, and they can roughly set prices together, then they are going to grant wage increases together, and they are going to turn those wage increases over into higher prices for consumers. You buy industrial price, everybody rises together, the rising tide basically lifts all boats, and there is a fair degree of job stability, though not much innovation, not much change, not much application of new technology. We used to joke about our automobiles that every year the fins got longer, but the stuff underneath the hood was pretty much the same.

This all began to change in the 1980s and 1990s. Partly, it was due to international competition; foreign manufacturers came to the United States. It was easier through technology, cargo ships, and containerized ships to buy things from anywhere around the world. Many services became digitized. It was possible for consumers to find out where they could get better deals from anywhere. It was not just globalization; it was also technology. Technology made a lot of high-volume, standardized work into commodities that could be replicated by machinery. We used to have live telephone operators, we used to have live bank operators, we used to have service stations. Can you imagine that? We used to have a lot of people both in manufacturing and services doing essentially the same thing over and over again, but because of technology and globalization, because of the enormous innovations that have occurred with increased competition, those jobs have vanished, and employment security has vanished. Companies are under enormous pressure now, because of intense competition, to get their cost structures down, and that means that they are laying people off at an extraordinary rate. The people who are being laid off most are what we might call the routine production workers, those workers who are in competition with both technology and workers abroad. They are losing their jobs. In the recession of 1990 and 1991, those jobs did not come back. Throughout the roaring 1990s, we lost and continued to lose a huge number of routine production jobs both in manufacturing and in the service sector. That is a very shorthand way of explaining to you what really is a very complicated process that has occurred over the past twenty to thirty years.

Question: So in a globalized economy, what should be the constitution and role of labor organizations around the world? How should they be built up?

RR: When I was secretary of labor, the administration wanted to get the North American Free Trade Act signed, sealed, and delivered. I talked to a lot of unionized audiences, many of them manufacturing workers who were losing their jobs, and I kept saying to them, "Look, the North American Free Trade Act is a little piece of a much larger picture. You are never going to be able to keep your jobs because of technological change and globalization. You are probably going to need new skills. Hopefully, your companies are going to retrain you, and hopefully, we are going to invest a lot more in retraining and in education and in economic development, but those old jobs are never coming back."

When I addressed the International Labor Organization (ILO) in Geneva, the big issue there was labor standards, and whether the United States should argue that every country has to treat its workers as well—and every business in every country should have to treat its workers as well—as American workers are treated. Is it appropriate to ask workers and companies in developing nations to be paid the same minimum wage as workers in the United States? What about working conditions? Should safety regulations be exactly the same as in the United States?

My discussions with the ILO essentially resulted in a compromise. You see, if we asked every developing nation to have the same worker standards and the same minimum wage as workers in the United States, then many countries could not afford those. It would be a kind of back-door protectionism. In fact, many developing nations were afraid that that was exactly what we were going to do. They were afraid that we were going to use the fact that they paid very low wages and provided less safe or less environmentally sustainable working conditions as an argument for not trading with those countries. Essentially the compromise we came to was this: there shall be internationally no slave labor, no forced labor, and no labor of children under the age of twelve, and the United States will do whatever it possibly can to prevent these things, even if it may mean loss of trade. We also do want to guarantee the right of free association for workers in every nation to come together and form labor unions. But with regard to minimum wage and working conditions, we are going to ask countries, as they get wealthier, to improve their wages and working conditions. We understand that not every country can afford to treat its workers exactly the same as the United States. But as you become wealthier, largely through trade, we expect that your minimum wage will go up, we expect that your median wage will go up, we expect that your working conditions will continually improve. And we will monitor those things.

Question: What about U.S. corporations going abroad for sweatshops? The working conditions might be atrocious in our eyes, but in those countries the companies might actually help the workers and those workers might actually want to work there.

RR: It is very easy to define what a sweatshop is in the United States. If you simply say they are getting a small portion of the minimum wage and they are in unsafe working conditions, those would make my definition of a sweatshop. Not only do we have to close them down, but we also have to make sure that major manufacturers and retailers take responsibility for policing their subcontractors. That is what we tried to do.

What about, you ask, places around the world where workers are being paid a small fraction of American wages and they are not as safe? The answer is that a lot of it depends on the standard of living in that country. We cannot expect every country to be up to American standards, but we can put pressure—not only through trade, but through the IMF, through aid—to make sure that a country provides its workers with a minimally adequate standard of living relative to what that country can afford. Again, a minimum wage might be one-half the median wage; that might be a rule of thumb. You point out something that is not often discussed. If you have children who are working at a small fraction of American wages, and you do not trade, and you tell that country "You must not do that, you cannot employ fourteen-year-olds six days a week," those fourteen-year-olds might find their way into prostitution or even worse working conditions. We need to provide those countries with the ability to get those fourteen-year-olds into schools and raise living standards so they do not have to be in factories working six days a week.

Question: Earlier, you said if we do not get involved in the political process, we are letting the other guys win. I guess the question is, Where are our guys? You wrote an article about how we have had increased military spending and increased tax cuts that have largely benefited just the wealthy and will hurt the lower and middle classes. Meanwhile, we have had very little dissent, and the dissent we have had has been generally ineffective. Where do people who want to be involved in the electoral process and the political process turn to have some sort of effective dissent? Where are our guys?

RR: I strongly believe that most Republicans and Democrats are disagreeing about means rather than ends. Some of us disagree about ends. But most of us, Republicans or Democrats, would object to a political system controlled by people with a lot of money—and that is what our political system has become. I set out to become governor of Massachusetts fairly naively. But what I did not do that I should have done is start much earlier and really develop a grassroots organization in the state. Massachusetts, unlike, for example, in California... Well, let me be careful what I say about California. I love California. I just returned last week from California. The climate is superior to Massachusetts. But California is a state in which electoral politics is won or lost on the basis of television advertisements; California is an air-war state. You have got to raise a huge amount of money. Gray Davis raised sixty million dollars and just basically obliterated his opponent. Essentially, he also selected his opponent. Gray Davis, a Democrat, decided that he did not want to run against Richard Riordan, a very moderate Republican who might have beat him. He ran advertisements during the Republican primary against the Republican who he thought had a better chance of beating him and made it possible for a much more conservative Republican to be his opponent. Now I suppose that this is legal, but, to me, it violates the spirit of what our democracy is all about.

In Massachusetts and some other states, it is still possible to have a ground war through grassroots organizing and to run a campaign that is based upon both the Internet and people talking to each other. I went around this state town by town, city by city, and spoke at town meetings. I think if I had done it for another year, I might have won. I did not have the money, but I did spend five hours a day on the telephone, calling everybody I could think of asking them to contribute money to my campaign so that I could have a little bit of an air war. But the winner, Mitt Romney, ultimately spent 12 million dollars, and something like 4, 5, or 6 million of the 12 million came from his own pocket. We cannot have a democracy that is dominated by rich people who are basically paying for themselves. Nor can we have a democracy that is basically run by big companies and even big labor or any big organizations that are financing campaigns.

Now, where does that leave you? Where it leaves you is, if you want to be involved in politics at the grass roots, there is still plenty of room. Even California I would not give up on. I think we have got to revive grassroots politics in this country. I think that is the only way of combating these air wars unless we get campaign finance reform, clean elections reform, and some public financing of air-war campaigns. But that is no replacement for grassroots campaigning.

Question: Could you say a bit more about the experience of your gubernatorial campaign? For many of us, you struck us as a person of enormous hope, someone who would keep going no matter how badly things went. What does it feel like to be in electoral politics for the first time and see the way that large amounts of money can bulldoze ordinary citizens who are trying to make a difference? How did you maintain hope?

RR: Look, I survived Bill Clinton's cabinet. I survived Washington when the Republicans took over Congress. Washington, folks, is the kind of city where a friend is somebody who stabs you in the front. I am eternally optimistic and positive because people out there are enormously idealistic. How many of you have taken an introductory economics course? What microeconomics leaves out is that we carry around in our heads aspirations for the common good. It is not only aspirations for what we want for ourselves, but we also have ideals about what is good for our society, what is good for the world. These aspirations—whether we call them the public interest, the common good, or something else —are the stuff of which politics really should be made. And you can tap into them.

The best thing about being a politician was traveling around Massachusetts. In fact, even when I was in Bill Clinton's cabinet traveling around the country and talking to people, we talked not only about their own needs—health care, child care, better schools, pension reform—but also their aspirations for what other people needed. I remember when we tried to raise the minimum wage in 1995 or 1996 for the first time in years, most people in Washington told me, "There is no way you are going to get public support for this because the minimum wage touches just a small fragment of the workforce. It is an old democratic theme nobody cares about." Well, it turns out that 85 percent of Americans thought the minimum wage ought to be raised. Many of them felt very passionate about it. We steamrolled a Republican Congress because they had so much mail from so many people saying this is the only right and decent thing to do.

I could give you a lot of other examples having to do with workforce safety. Sweatshops. When one of our inspectors found Kathy Lee Gifford labels on some garments in a sweatshop in New York City, I knew that that was going to be the edge of the wedge in terms of getting a lot of people involved because we did not want to wear garments made by people earning a tiny, tiny fraction of the minimum wage in conditions that would make you blanch.

If you want to get into politics, people want to hear aspirations about the common good. People also want to behold and vote for somebody who has integrity. They might not agree with everything that that person says. You may not agree with everything that the late Paul Wellstone stood for. In fact, Paul Wellstone came out against the Iraqi war resolution. We talked on the phone right afterwards. I said, "Well how do the people in Minnesota feel about that?" He said, "Well, most of them think that I am wrong, but I am still going to win this fight." John McCain is exactly the same. John McCain is somebody about whom people say, "Well, I do not believe in everything he stands for, but I believe he is standing up for what he believes, and that is important to me."

Question: You spoke about having labor associations across boundaries. What do you think of the argument that some of the great economic disparities between the U.S. and other countries result from the fact that we allow resources to move among countries but not labor? Would you suggest that labor boundaries be opened up so that people can move to places where there are jobs and their work is needed and properly rewarded?

RR: I am basically in favor of broadening immigration to this country. But let's not fool ourselves. Inequality of income and wages, and you might also say opportunity, is widening in the United States and in almost every other country. At the top in the United States and every other country, you are finding very well-educated people. Computer engineers in India are earning less than computer engineers in the United States, but they are still earning really reasonable middle-class wages even by American standards. Increasingly, it is a global labor market in which the better-educated people who can solve and identify and manipulate symbols and solve and identify problems are doing better and better. They are lawyers, investment bankers, marketers, engineers, and designers, and the demand for them is increasing. But if they are routine workers engaged in routine operations, they are in competition with people from all over the world and technology, and their wages are dropping. Many of the people who had been in routine manufacturing are finding themselves in the local service economy—retail, restaurant, hotel, hospital, attention-giving services like child care or home health care—and these jobs do not pay very much. This is where a lot of the new jobs are opening in the United States for people without college degrees. It is not all that different in Europe. It is really becoming not all that different in many other countries that we were considering, a few years ago, to be developing nations.

So the answer to your question is yes. More immigration—

fine. But that is not going to solve the problem of widening inequality here and all over the world.

Question: In e-mails that circulated after your gubernatorial campaign, you talked a lot about reinvigorating the Democratic Party. I was wondering what your thoughts were for changes that need to be made to reinvigorate the Massachusetts Democratic Party and also the national party, and what you see as a future that will lead the Democratic Party to more success in elections.

RR: First of all, let me say that there really is not a Democratic Party. There is not much of a Republican Party, but there is even less of a Democratic Party. There is a sump pump called the Democratic National Committee that is a financial sump pump. Basically, it goes out and sends out mass mailings and it brings money in, and then it distributes that money to a lot of entrepreneurial candidates, each of whom is doing their own money raising. The Democratic Party, as a party—if you think of a party as parties used to be—has state parties, state conventions, hundreds of thousands of people involved. They come to a national convention. They are the kind of ground troops I was alluding to before. That is not the Democratic Party today. The Republican Party is a little bit more of a party because the Republicans traditionally are a little more disciplined than the Democrats, but there is not much of a grassroots Republican Party either. There is an oligarchy. And that oligarchy, for example, decided in the year 2000 that George W. Bush would be the nominee in the next election. If you have an oligarchy, you can get a lot done pretty easily.

Here is what we need to do—and I am saying *we*. I do not care whether you are a Republican, a Democrat, a Green, or an independent; I do not care who you are. But *we*, we as Americans who are interested in taking politics back and democracy back, what we have to do is get serious in working at—I am going to repeat myself but I want to extend the theme a little bit— at the grass roots. What do I mean by working at the grass roots? You now live in Cambridge, Massachusetts. You are a citizen of Cambridge. Saturday, there was a caucus in Cambridge with regard to going to the state party and an upcoming issues convention. Now, there were students at that caucus—quite a number. I am delighted to say that many of them got involved in local politics through my campaign. Could there have been more, and would it have made any difference for more of you to be there? It might have, at the margin, made some more difference. You might have met more people involved in local politics and felt your own power. That is the essence of involving yourself in politics.

A year ago, many college students went to the caucuses when the caucuses counted for more because we were, a year ago, deciding on who was going to go to the state convention to nominate people to be the Democratic nominee for governor. And many of the students who went to the caucuses came back and e-mailed me and said, "We took over the X caucus or the Y caucus. We took over ward three. We nominated each other. We are going to the state convention. We are representing blank or blank. We feel more powerful and politically efficacious than we ever felt before. We did not know it was so easy." Well, it is not always that easy. But to feel politically powerful, to understand that the democratic process really can respond to you is a heady and very important understanding.

JULIET SCHOR, economist

As an economist, Juliet Schor has focused public attention on a trend that many Americans know from personal experience: overwork. Her best-selling book The Overworked American: The Unexpected Decline of Leisure *finds that Americans now spend more hours working than at any time since World War II. Schor's subsequent writings have shed light on the culture of consumerism and its relationship to family, women's issues, economic justice, and environmental sustainability. Schor is professor of sociology at Boston College as well as a cofounder and board member of the Center for a New American Dream, an organization devoted to transforming North American lifestyles through responsible consumption. In this interview, Schor paints a vivid portrait of a consumer society fueled by advertising that leaves many overworked Americans feeling depressed. She describes alternative policies that would offer workers more choice as well as her own efforts to limit the market's influence on her children.*

Question: While people in the U.S. become increasingly overworked, there seems to be a pressing need to help those struggling at the very bottom. How do you think people gain a sense of social responsibility? What personal experiences have given you a sense of this social responsibility?

Juliet Schor: The growth of the need to help those "at the very bottom" comes from the fact that over the past twenty years the conditions of life for people at the bottom in this country have gotten worse. If you look at the big picture, what has happened in this country is a dramatic shift from the first post–World War

II period, roughly 1945 to 1975, in which, as a society, we were becoming more equal. Conditions of life were improving, with increased access to health care, education, and basic services. Then we have a turnaround. Income distribution begins to worsen in the 1970s. Government policy turns sharply against the poor beginning in 1980 and toward a society that creates more privilege for a small group of people.

The dominant approach out there when it comes to issues of social responsibility is service and volunteering—coming out of traditions of *noblesse oblige,* the duty of the wealthy to help the poor. There are also traditions that address these issues from the point of view of doing what is socially just in which each of us has our own obligation or role in terms of making society a more just and ethical place. It is the second tradition that I personally believe in and that I worry is being crowded out by the first. The thing about the first is that it essentially leaves structures of privilege in place; it says in a world in which some people have so much, it is their duty to give a little more to the people below. It does not question the basic structures that lead to extremes of privilege and situation.

As to your question of how I got there personally, when I was nine years old, I liked Nelson Rockefeller, who ran for president. He was a Republican. But the Vietnam War had already begun, and of course it was starting to radicalize people who were conscious of what was going on then. I will not say that I was radicalized by the Vietnam War, although I went to protest marches and was involved in the movements of the 1960s. I was politically active in high school. My first cause was the United Farm Workers' Union, a group of unorganized and very oppressed migrant workers, mostly from Mexico, who were being exploited by the

growers, mostly in California. Truth be told, although I did not
know it growing up, my parents were both Communists, and I
think that is how I ended up the way I am. I found out when I was
in high school. When they tried to control my political activity,
they had to come clean about their own. I am sure, in whatever
subtle ways they transmitted it to me, that is where it came from.
By the way, in the era they were Communists, it was a much bigger movement and was fighting for a lot of the things that liberals came to fight for—racial integration, economic justice, union
rights, the rights of workers, the rights of women. It was very different than what we think of as Communist today.

Question: Why did you decide to research New Consumerism? Was
there a moment during your youth or education that significantly raised your concern about it?

JS: I got into it by accident, actually, later in life. When I came
to Harvard in 1984, I had a standard economist's view about
consumption issues, which was that more is better. It is a simple story: we should grow as fast as we can, and we can solve environmental problems through technology. Also, as a radical
economist coming out of a Marxian economic tradition, I focused more on production. (Historically, Marxists have tended
not to think too much about consumption, particularly in fields
like economics.) I ended up completely revising my views and
arriving at a very different point of view after first researching
the workplace.

My book *The Overworked American* is almost all about the
workplace, the pressure on workers to work longer hours and
why people were not getting more leisure time. Despite incredible growth of productivity in our society, what I found as I
started looking at the data was that workers were actually work-

ing longer hours. That left an interesting question about the income that people were getting and what they were doing with it, and why in surveys asking workers about the tradeoff between money and free time most people said they pretty much liked what they had and did not show dissatisfaction about hours of work. What I started to do was examine the spending side of it, because I thought that must be important in understanding why people are satisfied with the fact that they are working longer hours. I developed what I called the model of work and spend. What I found was that people's preferences about money and consumption adapt to what is happening in their lives. When surveys asked workers if they would rather have a raise or more free time, very large numbers of workers said they preferred the free time. But the system did not give that to them, giving income instead. They spent the income and became habituated to that kind of spending. When pollsters would go back a year or two later and ask the same questions, people would again say they were happy with what they had. I argue that that happened again and again in the post–World War II era.

This is the total reverse of the standard argument, which says people have preferences for consumption. They exercise those in the market and get what they want. The standard argument also says that the number of hours people work is a reflection of their preferences, so they are choosing their hours of work and are again getting just what they want. What I argue is that the system works in reverse. Workers end up wanting what they have, so their preferences adapt to what is out there in the labor market. Given that there is a lot of rigidity in the system, workers have not had the opportunity to trade off productivity growth against leisure time. This relatively simple model just scratched the surface of the issue of consumption.

Question: In the news, we often hear consumerism linked with a better economy, for instance, during holiday shopping season. Do
you feel that is an accurate interpretation, that consumer spending is the foundation of a healthy economy? What do you think
motivates this depiction on news coverage?

JS: There is a difference between the possibilities for an economy
and the way the U.S. economy is currently structured. It is true
that in recent years especially we have shifted much more to
a consumer-driven economy and, in particular, a debt-driven
economy. A lot of that consumer spending is happening because
of debt. People work longer hours in part so they can pay debts
and keep up with these lifestyles. We have more and more activity and personnel devoted to marketing and advertising, with
increasing dollars going in that direction.

   People may remember after September 11th, when President
Bush came out and said that the thing people could do to be real
patriots was to go to the mall and shop. By the way, people did
not respond to this message for many reasons, one of which is
that many Americans have a tremendous amount of debt. Particularly with the economy crashing, they did not feel comfortable going out and adding more debt to their credit cards.

   When people like myself and organizations like the Center
for a New American Dream talk about issues concerning the relationship between consumerism and the economy, our view is
that there is a precariousness to this form of economy and it has
negative impacts we want to avoid, environmental impacts being
central among them. Also, if you think about what has happened
in this period that I call New Consumerism, which refers to the
last twenty years, especially since the 1990s, increasingly you
have money going towards luxury and status consumption and
away from the satisfaction of people's basic needs. We have an

increasing number of people who do not have health insurance
or access to good health care. We have our school budgets being
cut all around the country. We are shifting away from things like
education, health care, social services, high-quality food (as opposed to cheap, fast food)—these are all things research tells us
would do much more to give people well-being.

As a result, critics say we need to change the foundation of the
economy. It is not so much about spending less; it is about spending differently. Our economy has been on the path of the maxi-
mal rate of growth, of which much of that is consumption. There
are plenty of examples of other economies in which private consumption is a smaller fraction of total economic activity.

Let's say people agreed with me and wanted to do less of
this private consumption. If we try to cut back or try to change,
wouldn't the economy collapse? People worry a lot about that.
With the message that I am giving, people say, "Wait a second.
How can we have a healthy economy if people consume less?"
There are two ways to think about that: if every person in this
country cut up all his or her credit cards tomorrow and decided
to live with much more modest consumer spending, there is no
question that we would have an economic collapse. But that is an
unrealistic vision of how it would actually happen. The transformation would occur gradually and largely because people decide
they want to opt for more time out of the labor market, earn less
money, and therefore have to spend less since they are not going
to be earning as much. If you have a gradual shift to shorter
hours of work and downshifting in the labor market, you can actually shift to a different kind of economy without chaos and
unemployment.

Rather than urge people to go to the mall and buy more stuff that they do not really need, we should have taken the opportunity after 9-11 to pull together as a country and ask, "What are the things we in this country really need, to which we could devote time, energy, and money?" That, to me, would have been more patriotic and more like what happened after the Second World War. We need to rebuild schools, we need to fix our health care system, we need to fix our foster care system, we need to clean up our environment. These are urgent needs in this country. These are the needs to which we can devote time and money that will give us more well-being.

Question: How would you respond to your critics' claim that there seems to be an American cultural preference for income over leisure in terms of the willingness to work overtime? By what grounds do you quantify or measure quality of life and arrive at the conclusion that Europeans have it better than we do?

JS: Is it just a cultural phenomenon that Americans are long-hour workers? A very short time horizon might give you that point of view. But if you look fifty years back, after the Second World War, the U.S. had much shorter working hours than Europe. We eliminated Saturday work and went to a forty-hour standard workweek long before Europe did. That mostly had to do with the fact that our GNP was growing faster in the early part of the century. We were getting wealthier quicker.

You can see the same thing with Japan. When I started doing this research, Japan was the world's workaholic nation. We have now surpassed Japan in terms of working hours. There was a lot of talk about how overwork was deep in the Japanese psyche and culture, which would not allow them to work shorter hours. However, decades earlier, the stereotype of the Japanese was that they were a ne'er-do-well, lazy culture. We have to be careful about culture and ascribing too much to it, particularly when we are seeing very big changes in working hours in very short periods of time. Those are probably not going to be caused by culture shifts or cultural determinants.

The more important factors have to do with some of the economic factors that are driving hours of work. One is the way in which employers have pushed the norm to higher work hours. Surveys looking at changes in work over the last twenty-five years show that employees report not only working many more hours, but also their intensity of work has increased. The expansion of work into private time has increased. There are some very specific driving factors for this in the U.S., for example, the demise of the trade union movement, which was the key driver of shorter hours of work before World War II. Unions are still a major factor in Europe, which explains why European working hours have fallen and American working hours have turned around. There is also no doubt that there is a history in this country of the so-called Protestant work ethic and that the U.S. has been consumerist, leading the world in the development of mass consumerist culture.

The second question was about Europe and quality of life. What is quality of life, and why do I say that Europeans have a higher quality of life? Here I am taking a conventional view of quality of life in terms of the way it has been defined in social science research. Social scientists actually now know a fair amount about what gives people well-being, in both subjective and objective terms. We know that healthy social relations are absolutely central to people's well-being. Strong friendships, strong connections with family, strong community ties—those are key determinants of having both high objective well-being (as measured by a variety of factors like mental and physical health) and also subjective well-being (people's own reports of how happy they are, how good they feel). Healthy intimate relationships, good health, a sense of meaning in life—these things are all very strong determinants of well-being.

Working long hours, watching a lot of television, shopping a lot, having materialist values—those things do not contribute very much to well-being. In some cases, they undermine well-being. For example, let's take consumerist values. There is now a very extensive literature in psychology which shows that the more materialist you are, the more you care about accumulating stuff, the more you care about making money, the more priority you give to possessions and financial success over other things, the worse off you are. You are more likely to be depressed. You are more likely to be anxious. You will have lower self-esteem. You are also more likely to have stomachaches, headaches, and psychosomatic illnesses. You will have less of what psychologists call "life vitality." There is a lot of literature on adolescents and adults that shows this. Consumerist values are just not a healthy value system.

I have just completed analyses on middle-school children, asking similar kinds of questions—measuring how involved they are in consumer culture, how much they care about having stuff and labels, and how much television they watch. Then I took measures of their well-being, such as their levels of anxiety and depression, how often they get stomachaches and headaches, how bored they are, what they think of their parents, and their levels of self-esteem. All of those psychological outcomes are adversely affected by involvement in consumer culture; the kids who are more into this culture score lower on all of those

psychological measures. An underlying causal model shows that
it is their involvement in consumer culture that causes all of
those things; it is not the other way around where "screwed up"
kids gravitate towards consumer culture.

Here is one more point on that: research also shows that the
more television and other forms of media you watch, the more
consumer involved you are. Children who watch a lot of TV and
use other media are more likely to care about money, stuff, and
labels and to worry about how much they have relative to other
people. That, by the way, is key here. One of the real secrets to
well-being is not to worry too much about having less than other
people. The more oriented you are to comparing yourselves to
others, the lower you are going to score on all of these outcome
variables—more depression and anxiety and lower self-esteem.
I found this in a lot of research that I have done in different
areas.

Question: In *The Overspent American* you identify not just adults
but also children as suffering from a need to constantly compare their own material possessions to those of their peers. As a
mother, how do you cope with your own children's desire or need
to fit in?

JS: I guess my kids will not mind if I talk about them in front of six
hundred people. I have two children. One is twelve, a boy. One
is eight, a girl. When my son was born, we decided to start him
off without any television. It was not that I felt dogmatic about
this, saying, "I could never let my child watch television. It is
such a bad thing." I wanted to get reading and love of reading
well established. With young people today, there is so much electronic media that we are in danger of not reproducing love of
reading, which is something that my parents gave to me and is

really valuable, both as an entertainment and a critical skill. That was my thinking at the beginning: get him really into reading, and then if he wants to watch television, that is fine. Why was I worried about reading? The research says that for kids who watch TV early on, it is harder to become good and avid readers, through a pushing-out effect. I was less worried about the impact of television on cognitive achievement and other things.

People were hostile to me about this, by the way. They got defensive. People constantly warned me how hard it was going to be when I would no longer be able to control my child, and how he was going to turn into a TV addict. I figured, when he asks for it, I'll give it to him. I did not want TV to become a point of contention or a forbidden fruit.

My son was five years old when he asked about it. I said, "We do not think television is very good for you," and discussed why. He took it pretty seriously and then never really asked to watch after that. Recently, occasionally, he can watch a sports event or something like that. My second child basically followed in the wake. We have been able to raise our children basically television free. Of course, my husband and I had to stop watching television. You cannot do it in a hypocritical way. It has worked out really well; the kids are great at entertaining themselves.

It has also been positive in avoiding the "I want this, I want that" syndrome and all the advertising that is beamed at kids through television. I have just finished a book on the commercialization of childhood, the growth of marketing to children, and their increasing immersion in consumer culture. You have to be really careful in this culture about how much media you watch and how much you let it define your inner life. *The Overspent American* talks about how people who watch more televi-

sion spend more money and save less. I argue that it has to do
with the impact that television has on our lifestyle desires. Like
any other thing, it influences people, and we have to be conscious, aware, and proactive about it, rather than passive. Something like 57 percent of U.S. households are what are called
"constant television households," in which the TV is on all the
time. Although that does not mean people are glued to the TV
all the time, there is a way in which television has become a constant backdrop in our society. That is something we have to pay
attention to.

Overall, my view is that we are trying to create a positive culture in our household and with our friends because you need to
do it in a larger community, too. If your kids are always socializ-
ing with people whose values and practices you do not like, you
are going to have problems. You want to put them in a context of
people who share, to some extent, values and practices you want
to reproduce for your children.

This is not just about raising children television free; it is
about giving our kids the sense that we believe in something.
There is a positive aspect to it as opposed to merely a "You can't
do this, you can't do that" mentality, which is all about restricting. My husband and I want to create a cultural environment for
our children that gives them what we feel is healthy, positive,
stimulating, and creative.

Question: In an interview in Z *Magazine,* you say that we need to organize to change American work hours. What strategies of organization would be most effective? Where have organizing efforts
around work hours fallen short in the past?

JS: If you look at the post–World War II period in union organizing
around work time, what you see is very little progress. There

were a few contracts in some of the big manufacturing industries which gave more personal days, so there was a little movement there. But for the most part, this has been a nonissue in the second half of the twentieth century and continuing now into the twenty-first century.

Historically, in the period right after World War II, the unions that articulated a strong agenda for shorter hours were unions with large numbers of women. It is not hard for us to figure out why that is. One issue that has come up in the literature is the idea that if men's jobs were shorter, they would have to do more work at home. That is a less appealing alternative than working longer hours. That is the first point: look for the larger number of women workers who are more time pressed because demands in the household economy are higher, creating much higher levels of total working hours.

Point two: the labor movement, not only on this issue but all issues, can no longer achieve much on its own. It is weak and small. What they are trying to do now is just fend off attacks. The Bush administration is trying to reduce hours protections and make it easier for firms to demand longer hours from workers. The movement has to reach out to groups who are concerned about family, who care about children's well-being, who are concerned about the environment—the impact of long hours, fast growth, and a high-consumption economy on the environment. By identifying common causes around relevant issues, the labor movement will be able to make a bigger impact.

Another way in which people have been organizing to change work hours is through groups like the Center for a New American Dream, which I helped to found in 1995. In a short period of time, we have grown from nothing to a staff of more than twenty people around a message of what you might call ecological and social sustainability. By social sustainability, we are talking about patterns of time use of working and consuming, which make it possible for us to reproduce not only a well-functioning and successful economy but also healthy families and communities. We have a growing number of people who are resonating to our message and getting active. For instance, there is now a voluntary simplicity movement, which has grown very rapidly. Similar groups have also formed around the country. On April 6, 2003, we had the official start of a movement called Take Back Your Time Day, which celebrates a day of nonwork on October 24. If Americans had the working hours of Western Europeans, October 24th would be the last day of the year that we would work. On average now, Americans work nine weeks *more* than the typical German, French, Dutch, or Nordic employee. Those are some examples of social movements that are developing to try and move our cultures in the directions I am talking about.

Question: While your idea about cutting back on work hours makes sense theoretically, how would you carry this out in practice? What would you say to somebody who wants to live lavishly and is willing and eager to work more hours and make more money, or to someone who needs money for their family especially in professions like law enforcement, where overtime hours make up a large part of the salary?

JS: Very much at the center of my vision of reducing work time is giving people choice. The way the labor market is structured right now, you have a choice to take a job or not to take a job. But once you have a job, most employees have relatively low flexibility to reduce their hours within that job.

For example, I did a survey at a major corporation in which I asked people, "How feasible is it within your current position to reduce your hours?" Eighty-five percent said it was fairly difficult or impossible. For the most part, what we have is a market in which hours of work are tied to jobs. Economists have done research on this, and they find that when people want to change their hours of work, they typically have to change their jobs.

In part, what I am arguing for is the opening up of a market. We do not have a well-functioning market in hours. It is easier to get more hours, but it is very hard to find good jobs in this economy where you can work shorter hours if you want to. It is very hard to reduce your hours for a while because you want to spend time with your family or pursue another interest and then be able to increase them again. This is a huge problem for women, many of whom have to leave jobs when they have children and cannot get back into those jobs again. You have a stymied career path in many jobs if you want to work shorter hours.

If you look at the career trajectories of men and women, it is still the case that you have a huge gap in earnings. It no longer happens right after college. In the years right after college, men and women do pretty equivalently in terms of wage gap and career mobility. But when women have children, their careers pretty much flatten out and men's continue to rise in terms of income and promotions. A big part of why that happens is that women can no longer devote very long hours to their jobs as they did before they had children. That then leads to dead-ending in their careers.

Finally, there is the question of how to get there. There is a highly articulated desire among employees now in this country to work shorter hours, to trade income for time. We can do it through financial incentives to firms. We can do it through legis-

lation. There are a whole series of policies that would move us
in the direction of giving people more ability to trade money
for time. For example, the Netherlands passed a law a couple of
years ago which said that anybody who wanted to reduce hours
at their job would have the right to do so. The employer would
need to give them the opportunity to work shorter hours. We can
do it by shifting the fair labor standards in the way that I just
talked about either by going to a lower standard workweek—
which, by the way, does not prevent people from working more;
it only prevents firms from forcing them to work more—or by
outlawing mandatory overtime. There are very few employees
in this country who have the right to say no to overtime hours.
That seems to me a right that people should have in this country.
They should not face losing their job if they do not want to work
fifty or sixty hours a week, which is what many manufacturing
workers face.

Question: In an interview with David Barsamian, you contrast a typical American's idea of leisure time, such as TV watching and
shopping, to higher-quality leisure activities and the idyllic notion of passing time, which we see in places such as southern Europe. Can improving the quality of our leisure time simply mean
increasing its quantity so that people can make better use of
it? Do you believe there is also significant cultural change or
a change in our values that must occur before Americans will
change their behavior?

JS: Part of what has happened is that our leisure time has become
less satisfying and less vibrant as working hours have risen.
There is a connection between the way we structure our work
sphere and our leisure. In countries where people work more
hours, they also watch more television, other things being equal.

We are less likely to engage in activities that require big investments of time.

However, research has shown that the kinds of leisure activities that require big blocks of time and require developing skills are the ones that give the most back to people and are most satisfying. For example, getting involved in a local theater group or learning how to play an instrument well, getting into a band, developing your skills in woodworking or art—those are the more active kinds of leisure activities that yield the highest process benefits. Long and unpredictable work schedules make it much harder to commit to doing those activities because you have less time. One thing we find in studies of people who have a four-day workweek is that they will never go back to the five days because they change the way they live. It is a very useful form of leisure, and it allows people to engage in really satisfying leisure-time activities.

It is important to know that this is not just about my opinion or the kind of life that I prefer to lead. If we think about what has been happening in this country, we have extraordinary increases in depression and other forms of mental distress. We have a breakdown of community. We have high levels of family dissolution. We have children who are at risk in a variety of ways related to mental, physical, and emotional distress. We have kids committing suicide at record levels. All of those things are connected to these basic choices of working and spending—the way we are organizing our daily life, the way in which our economy is connecting with our families and community. Millions and millions of Americans are articulating a sense that their lives are out of balance, and they are searching for meaning. The value system of the 1990s—that economics is everything, making money is everything—is a value system that we rushed head-long into. Now, as we can look back with the benefit of research, we see this yields a lot of problems and does not, in the long run, yield satisfying and meaningful lives. We need to go back to the quality of life that facilitates our connections to each other, our connections to the earth, our ability to have healthy spiritual lives, and our ability to have a set of values and to live our daily life in accord with those values.

If I can give you any advice as you think about these issues, it is to stay true to the things that you really believe in, and to make life choices that allow you to do that. Do not sell your soul for some other purpose. Do something that you believe is really right. You will be much better off in the long run, aside from what it does for the world.

AARON FEUERSTEIN, corporate leader

Aaron Feuerstein is the former president and CEO of Malden Mills, the Massachusetts business that produces the innovative fabric Polartec. In 1995, when a fire ravaged much of his textile factory, Feuerstein became a media hero, the symbol of a socially responsible business owner who leads according to his conscience. Despite overwhelming pressure to resume operations overseas, Feuerstein pledged to rebuild the mill at home and pay his employees during the three-month reconstruction, a decision that ended in bankruptcy in 2001. Through it all, Feuerstein has been steadfast in his commitment to the local worker and his homegrown company, and he continues to fight against proposals to restructure and outsource labor to international markets. In this interview, Feuerstein discusses his own story and outlines a vision of social responsibility in corporate governance. These ideas were presented when Feuerstein was CEO, and they represent the strategy that would be followed should he succeed in buying back the company. They do not represent the philosophy of Malden Mills' current owners.

Question: You have often spoken about how your religious beliefs factored into your decision in 1995 to rebuild Malden Mills after a fire destroyed them. How large a role has religion played in your thought process?

Aaron Feuerstein: I was brought up in a very religious environment. It was liberally religious in that they did not believe that religion should have power over the state. They believed in separation of church and state. I gained many values, which have stayed with me for life.

I can mention one. The family used to eat together every night. I considered it an honor. Some of the other members of the family who considered it mandatory, which it was, didn't consider it such an honor. My parents and my siblings were there, and we used to discuss everything—school, religion, politics, etc. It was wonderful. I recall when I was a kid, my father spoke of how, when he was fourteen years old, he started working for his father in the Malden Mills, which was incorporated in 1906. He observed that my grandfather, who started the business, would go around every evening at around sunset as the work was over and pay each worker in accordance with his wages. My father said you don't really do that here in the United States; what you do is keep your records in such a way that the wages, the hours, the union benefits, and the taxes can be calculated. The only way that can be done is to pay in arrears the following week. My grandfather screamed out, "No, it's against the Torah, it's against the Bible." The next day, after public school (I was in a public school in Brookline), I had my Hebrew lessons with my maternal grandfather. I told him the story. I asked, "How is it possible that the Bible would be in opposition to paying in arrears?" He said, "Yes, your grandfather is right. It's in the Bible." He opened it up and showed me where it said (later I committed it to memory) you cannot oppress the working man because he's a poor man. You have to pay him each day. The sun cannot set on those wages because that is what sustains him [Deuteronomy 24:14–15]. Those kinds of values were talked about every day in the family.

Question: You appeal to a Jewish sense of ethics in your decision-making process. What guidelines would you recommend to those corporate decision makers who do not ascribe to a particular religion?

AF: Let me tell you what the mission is of Malden Mills, which is
     quite different than the mission of other corporations. The av-
     erage corporation in the United States has the primary mission
     to maximize the profitability of the shareholder. The CEO is re-
     minded of this every day because Wall Street is controlling the
     situation to the degree that the CEO is able to increase the value
     of the share for the shareholder. If the CEO is able to do it the
     very next quarter, to that degree his income is greatly improved.

     In our corporation, we have a mission statement, which states
     that we have many stakeholders. The shareholder in our corpo-
     ration, which is not public, happens to be my family. Yes, the
     profitability to the shareholder is very important. Without it,
     the business won't prosper. But there are other considerations as
     well which the CEO must keep in balance: we have responsibil-
     ity to the worker, both the union worker and the management
     worker, responsibility to the community, and responsibility to
     the environment. It's up to the CEO to keep these balanced. The
     CEO in our company cannot sacrifice the worker or the com-
     munity or the environment for the shareholder. That is the ma-
     jor difference.

     I really don't know what to do about public corporations so
     that they have mission statements like I have. I think in my small
     way, if I can manage to succeed—and when I say succeed, suc-
     ceed not only in my ideals but succeed financially—then it
     might awaken the realization in corporate America that, over
     the long term, a mission statement such as what we have will
     bring the best results. I do believe that.

Question: Why did you choose not to send your factories abroad,
     even if it could have given opportunities to workers that they
     have never had before, in addition to saving you money?

AF: Malden Mills is a global corporation. We have a plant in eastern

Germany in Görlitz, which is on the border between Poland and Germany. We have an arrangement in China with a plant in Shanghai. Our conception of the global work is that the plant in Europe will better serve its customer because it is located there and can handle the situation better than we can by producing and exporting products all over there, even though we do a great deal of export. As our new products mature, we want them to be made in Europe where they are being sold.

The same is true in Asia. The average corporation thinks that Asia is where the entrepreneur has the freedom to get labor at one dollar an hour instead of eighteen dollars an hour in the United States. Then they send the product back to the retail shop in the United States and get a greater profit margin. We do not think of it that way. We think of Asia for Asians. Asia has a big economy, and it is growing very rapidly. We do quite a bit of business in the Pacific Rim. We are going to use our Asian plant in order to gain a large share of the business that is available there. The only part of our Asian plant that we would use to bring product back into the United States would be product that would not take away from our operations in Lawrence and Methuen, Massachusetts.

I would like to say a little bit more on that point because it is critical. I could almost make a speech over that point. The plan that we have improves the manufacturing base of the United States and possibly can give a livable wage to the worker. When you have a manufacturing company making a product, the worker usually gets a wage that is livable, which gives him self-respect and with which he can bring up a family and see that his children are educated. When he loses that job, as the manufacturing base leaves the United States, the employment figures show that he or she usually finds a job in the service industry. In the majority of cases, that service industry job is close to the minimum wage and not a livable wage. You are substituting a respectable wage for one that is not. In fact, you are really increasing the spread between those who are entrepreneurs—those who are marketers and financial people and creative people—and the working class. The difference between a CEO's wages and the wages of a union worker, that distance keeps expanding. But if we continue with this business of removing the manufacturing base from the United States, it is going to get worse, and it is getting worse. Very possibly, the United States could end up as a second-class nation.

Question: What do you think of the idea of worker ownership, the idea that workers should collectively control the workplace and make decisions about production, and the idea that even in a unionized plant, workers have some say in workplace decisions, that their rights and dignity can't be fully realized as long as they have to rent themselves to someone who manages them and profits from their labor?

AF: I agree with that point of view. Until now, we have only gone as far as being respectful to our union. Unlike other textile mills, we do not think that the workers don't have the right to be represented by a union. I consider that very undemocratic. We have a union. In fact, we never have a strike with our union. The next step is to permit the workers to have not merely a stake as workers but also as shareholders. We are working on various plans, and someday I hope that might be a reality. It makes sense. When we do it, we are not going to do it exclusively for the CEO because we are a private family. We do not have to worry about what is happening to the share price. We would have many peo-

ple in the company participate; both management and union labor participate in being owners and in presenting ideas on how
the company can be creative and grow.

Question: In 1996 you told *Parade* magazine, "I have a responsibility to the worker and an equal responsibility to the community."
Do you ever feel that these social responsibilities clash with your
current business as a supplier of materials to the armed forces
and to hunting stores? Is your business, while you may not be
selling guns, not an accessory to the perpetual glamorization of
weapons, arms, and all things military in America?

AF: Thank you. Very good. In our case, the military amounts to 5
to 10 percent of our business. We are not making guns, even
though I am not necessarily a pacifist. We are not making the
guns; nor are we making the tanks. What we are doing is working with Natick Laboratories to make our soldier in the field
more comfortable and suffer less. Some of the new things that
we are working on with Natick Laboratories, pioneering textiles
and electronics, actually keep the soldier alive. We think that is
the way to go: to spend our money on research and development,
and not always make just the mature textile. We want to make
something that has more performance. So we are working on
special kinds of textile materials, which will report back to the
medic the heart rate of the soldier or the victim who has been
shot, to indicate if he is alive, or if he is not alive. In that way, we
have a good chance of keeping the wounded soldier alive. We
also have a good chance of keeping the medic alive, because every time you have special operational forces, you have a group
of medics who have to go out and service them. Many of them
get shot as they go out because they do not know whom to go to
first, whom they have a chance of saving, and who is already

gone. We also succeeded in making fire-resistant fleeces, which give warmth and ultimately keep the serviceman alive. Everything I am talking about also has eventual civilian applications. There are many disabled people and people who need help from textiles that can do more than just provide clothing for warmth. We are working on all of that, and we think it is important.

But to come to the key of your question: is it ethically wrong for us to be involved in something that is military? I maintain that, no, it is not. If we work with the American government to help defend our soldiers, then we are doing something worthwhile. The other thing that I would like you to know is that the military insists that any product that is made for them is made of American manufacture.

Question: You have often talked about having a responsibility to your workers. Do you think this responsibility should be universal for all employers? If so, should laws be passed to enforce this type of social responsibility even if it puts companies at risk?

AF: Oh, yes. If you had a movement in the United States that mirrored the mission statement of Malden Mills, you would not be losing your manufacturing base. You would not be losing the worker who gets a livable wage and forcing him to take a minimum wage. You would maintain the United States in its position as the number-one country in the world today.

Even though the question has not been asked, I would like to talk about economic justification. What economic justification is there to put in a mission statement "social responsibility"— responsibility to community, responsibility to worker, responsibility to the environment? What economic justification is there for that, and will it not, in the end, all be lost because it is not economically justifiable? We have given that a great deal of thought

at Malden. It started originally back after the Second World
War. While all the other textile mills were running down south
in order to save 20 to 30 percent on labor, we stayed in Lawrence.
We had to figure out then what to do. We slowly but surely
worked out a business strategy, which we think is economically
justifiable, so that a company can have a mission such as ours
and, at the same time, prosper.

There are three parts to it. Number one: we are determined
to make the very best quality we know how to make. We do not
stop until that quality is the very best in the world. We differentiate ourselves from the global commodity market, which does
not have that same kind of quality but fights for business on the
basis of price. The country that has the cheapest labor has the
best price and wins the ball game. We are not in that thing. We
differentiate ourselves from that. We insist on the best quality.

Number two: we commit our human and financial resources
to branding that quality. We have worked out a brand that is an
ingredient brand because we sell to people like Patagonia, North
Face, Lands' End, and L. L. Bean. It is a fabric that goes into
their products, so we call it ingredient. It is not the final product.
We want the consumer to know that the product he is buying in
the store is made of the best material, so we spend a great deal
of money building up our brand.

The third part of our strategy is financial and human resources devoted to research and development and innovation.
We think it is critical that a brand not live on its past history but
that a brand has to make its own products obsolete, as is being
done today in the electronic and high-technological fields. We
expect to do exactly the same thing so that what is going to be
copied of what we make offshore will not be the newest and
the best.

This strategy of quality, brand, and research and development makes a better textile fabric mill than ever before in U.S. history. We think that it is possible to accomplish this and to do so with a mission statement similar to ours.

Question: With the corporate scandals such as that involving Enron, what hope can you provide for us that you are not alone and that many in the business community are honest, kind people who care about more than just the bottom line?

AF: Theoretically, the CEO is supposed to take care of the bottom line and maximize the profitability of the shareholder at the expense of every other value. What actually happened in the case of Enron, and in some other cases, was that the CEO not only double-crossed the worker and the community and the environment but went one step further—he double-crossed his own shareholders. He was publicly declaring that he was taking care of the shareholder when in fact he was padding his own pocket at the expense of the shareholder. I always felt that it would come to that kind of an extreme because the average MBA student is taught that there is only one criterion for success, and that is maximizing profitability to the shareholder. Naturally, when he learns that in school, he goes out and is controlled by Wall Street, which tells him what to do. It had to happen that not only would he work for the shareholder, but he would also, in that kind of an environment, work for himself at the expense of the shareholder.

Question: Many of us admire not just your grit but also the grace with which you have handled very difficult situations, such as the factory fire in 1995. Where did you find the courage to act as you did, and where did you find the hope to sustain that courage?

AF: Wow. Well, it is very difficult to say where I found the courage. It was the right thing to do, and I always felt in business that do-

ing what is right is as important as making money. There should
not be a dichotomy, where it is dog-eat-dog during the day, charity is for one day a year at Christmastime and services in the
temple on Saturday, but the other six days you can do whatever
the hell you want. At that time, when the fire took place, it was
just before Christmas. There was no question that I was going to
rebuild, and I was going to rebuild right there. I was not going
to let the ideal and the objective that I had die because of a fire.
So we creatively schemed out how we could rebuild there. I
knew that I had positions for my maintenance people, who had
to rebuild the equipment, and for my construction people, who
had to rebuild the plants. But I did not have immediate employment for the union people who had to care for the equipment
and care for the production as it went through the production
line. I felt that that was not fair. Why should the union guy take
it on the neck a week before Christmas whilst the others who
were the more educated group and who were able to do other
things to help us get back into business, why should they get paid
and the union people not? And so it was maybe almost instinc-
tive that we went forward and paid the union people for ninety
days.

Question: Before your interview, you had mentioned that previous
to 1995 you had been a very private person, not in the public eye,
not giving talks on television. After the fire, you were suddenly
very much in the public eye, invited to all of the news programs.
That was a big change. Can you tell us what that was like to suddenly have an opportunity to address a wider public?

AF: Well, I do not think I really deserved the celebrity status that
I was thrown into. But it did help me. As a result of it, I have
widened my horizons; I am not insulated by the smallness of

my activity. For the question of whether I deserve that kind
of publicity...

Question: I didn't mean to be asking that.

AF: Well, I've got to ask that. The plant is located in the Arlington
Woolen Mill in Lawrence, Massachusetts, which is quite a big
complex. The original mill was built in 1865. Amazingly, when I
did some research, I found out that the original plant burned to
the ground the following year, in 1866. He rebuilt the way we
did. He stayed in the community. He did everything that he
should have done. He never received any of the publicity or
celebrity status that I got. I think it is a reflection of our time, that
maybe back then in the nineteenth century, caring for workers
and having a personal relationship with the community was
not considered abnormal to the degree that it is today. In the
twentieth century, with all our progress, it is considered very
abnormal. Therefore, this guy who did it, there has got to be
something special about him.

Question: Do you think that the workers in your factory work harder
than workers in factories where they are not treated so well?

AF: For the ninety-day payment, did the company get in return over
time? Yes, we got a great deal of return over time. I recall that
ten days after the fire, they called me up and they said that the
one plant, which remained intact, was able to make the Polartec
finished fabric. It was quite a miracle that it was operating because the workers went and refurbished that plant in ten days. It
would normally have taken any other company sixty or ninety
days. They invited me over, and I went over. I saw all the material coming off of the production line. I had not cried before. I
did not cry the night of the fire because crying weakens you so
you cannot think straight. But when I saw the material coming

off, it was just so wonderful that I realized that tears were coming to my eyes. I went up and down the production lines and shook hands with all the workers. The managers were all there as well, and they all had tears in their eyes.

There was one worker I will never forget who came over to me and he said, "Aaron, you don't have to thank us. I'm telling you, we're going to pay you back tenfold." And they did. They got us back into business very rapidly. In our textile business, it is so highly competitive that if you are out of the business for too many months, it is all over. They helped me there. They managed to get more production out with less equipment than we ever did before. They brought in a quality improvement that yields fewer seconds over a period of two years after the fire, which was amazing.

So there is no question in my eyes that the workers are an asset. They are playing a role in the business. It is not just how much you pay them. That is important. But it is what kind of work they are prepared to give you, and that is even more important. Over the long term, I think that will play a greater role than the amount of money you pay them.

NAOMI KLEIN, journalist

Once a self-described "mall rat" with an eye for designer labels, Naomi Klein today is a critic of corporate power and a leading light of the global justice movement. In 2000, at the age of thirty, Klein published No Logo: Taking Aim at the Brand Bullies, *a hotly debated critique of marketing's effects on culture and citizenship. Translated into twenty-five languages,* No Logo *was called by the* New York Times *"a movement bible." Klein has traveled throughout North America, Asia, Latin America, and Europe, documenting the rise of anticorporate activism for* The Nation, Newsweek International, *the* Globe and Mail, *and the* Guardian, *among other publications. Her book* Fences and Windows: Dispatches from the Front Lines of the Globalization Debate *tracks the globalization conflict from Seattle to September 11 and beyond. In this interview, Klein discusses campus activism, the North American way of life, and her role as an activist journalist in the anticorporate movement.*

Question: Between the moment you dropped out of college and the time when you finished writing *No Logo,* a book that would eventually be a global best seller, what were you doing? What were the steps that led you to create *No Logo,* and were the roots of that evident even in your time in college?

Naomi Klein: I was a student activist when I was at university; I studied philosophy and literature at the University of Toronto. But I got wrapped up in campus politics. I started writing for our university newspaper and ended up editing the paper, which is actually a full-time job. That is why I never completed my degree, because after I edited the student newspaper for a year, I got a student internship at the *Globe and Mail,* which is Canada's national newspaper, and they kept me on. So I tell my parents that it is really the *Globe's* fault that I did not finish my degree.

I was definitely an activist first, before I saw myself as a journalist. I started writing for the campus newspaper because I wanted to share with the rest of the university community why I was an activist. I also come from a political family—my mother was active in the women's movement—so you could say I inherited my interest in politics. Later, when I was working at a mainstream newspaper, I got really frustrated because they were not interested in covering the issues that I cared about. I went to a small progressive magazine in Canada and became editor of that magazine when I was about twenty-four. Out of the research I did for columns there as well as for other freelance writing, I decided to write *No Logo.*

The decision to write a book came from the realization that a lot of my research was connected. I realized that there was a connection between my interest in overmarketing and the loss of public space and my interest in the denigration of labor conditions. I had been writing about sweatshop conditions as well as corporate branding. I realized that these things were connected by a corporate ideology, but this was too big for an article. That is when I decided to write the book.

Question: Have you been able to instill a sense of urgency in other people who have been resigned to the issues surrounding globalization? How can students who feel powerless and resigned become active and help the fenced-in people you have written about who have been negatively affected by globalization?

NK: When I wrote *No Logo* in the late nineties, a lot of it was inspired by the student activism going on at that time. When I was in uni-

versity in the early nineties, the campus politics had very little to
do with macroeconomic issues. Nobody talked about globalization or the global economy. Very few people even talked about
the economy. The issues were very much focused on identity
and individual rights and group rights—not economic rights.
But when I think back on those years, there were some very key
global shifts happening in terms of the creation of the World
Trade Organization and loss of national power to trade agree-
ments and international organizations, as well as to private corporations through policies of privatization and deregulation.

When I think about what was driving us in those years, a lot
of it had to do with the battles around political correctness. We
were ill equipped to get our heads around something as huge
as the global economy. Unless you were specifically studying
international law, you did not learn about it at school. It was an
alphabet soup of acronyms that perpetually gave people the feeling that they were sick the day when everybody else learned
what all the acronyms stood for. In response to this, I think, we
kept focusing more and more inward—on ourselves, on our
campus, on our poor syllabus. But we somehow became so inward looking that we almost could not see the outside world of
our own campus, maybe our city—but certainly not our country, let alone the world. We became more and more parochial in
our concerns. Frankly, I think that had to do with a fear of actually confronting global economic issues and a feeling that we actually did not have the intellectual tools to do so.

The wave of activism that inspired me to write *No Logo* involved young people getting their heads around this incredibly
daunting structure by using the iconography of the global market itself. They would grab, say, a Nike running shoe and use it

as a popular education tool. They would follow the creation of this running shoe, where it was produced, how it was marketed, how it was sold at the mall, and then they had a picture, the X-ray, of the global economy in miniature. At the same time, by focusing on well-known brands, these issues connected to us in our culture because brands are pop culture icons as well as products. It was really about finding entry points: what you buy can be an entry point, what a school buys can be an entry point. So that is one answer to the question about how to bring a sense of urgency to these issues.

If you look at the rise of the anti-sweatshop movement and how it evolved, you see that students realized that labor injustices are not just happening in other countries; they are happening in our country and in our schools. At Harvard, we saw that with the very active Living Wage Campaign.

When people have an overwhelming feeling that the problem is so colossal they may as well just stay home and watch TV, they lose that sense of urgency. So you have to start small; you have to start personal. You can start with something that affects you, whether it is something that you buy, wear, or consume or whether it is the people who serve you—clean your rooms, serve you food, and pick the tomatoes for the fast food that you buy. We have all these personal connections to these huge issues, but there is no stopping there; we have to use these as entry points and then start talking about the policies and systems of power that make these injustices possible.

In terms of the urgency question, particularly in the United States, particularly on elite college campuses, there is so much privilege that we mistakenly believe that guilt is your best motivator. The way to get people active is to make them feel really bad and berate them with their complicity in an abusive system. That complicity is there and the abuses are there, but my experience is that guilt is a short-term motivator. Make people feel guilty and they might give money or sign a petition, but then they will just try to avoid the people making them feel guilty, because people really don't like to feel guilty.

But we do need to understand our complicity. I am going to Iraq in a couple of days, and my intention behind that trip is very clearly to shine a light on what the occupying powers in Iraq are doing and our complicity in that. At the same time, it is really important that when we talk about things like overconsumption and the role of the U.S. in the world that we also look at the promises of its lifestyle and whether it is actually making us happy. A war fought, in part, over oil, relates to the kind of isolated lives we live here as well as to climate change, from which no one is excluded. Arundhati Roy often asks people whether the so-called American way of life—a way of life so sacred and supposedly so wonderful that the government wages war around the world to protect it—actually makes them happy. She jokingly describes the American way of life as the right to live alone in your house with your washing machine, and when you put it that way it doesn't sound worth waging wars to protect.

A couple of years ago, I was speaking at an American campus right after living in Argentina for a year researching the economic crisis. I went straight from Buenos Aires to a university in Colorado. A young woman stood up to ask the first question. She said, "I understand what you are saying about Washington's neoliberal economic policies on Argentina, and I know it's really, really bad, but the problem is we do not really care, because we are comfortable." She said, "I have my own car and I drive to

Wal-Mart, to McDonald's, to school, and I am happy, so why should we care?" There are lots of ways that you can deconstruct that whole exchange. But what really struck me was that what she was describing—driving to Wal-Mart and McDonald's and driving to school, living from strip mall to strip mall—actually did not sound much fun. A lot of what we keep being told is this wonderful way of life that we have to protect is sometimes pretty bleak and lonely, which is why there are so many people on Prozac and other antidepressants.

Question: Your articles are obviously very opinionated and offer a particular view of politics. What do you believe to be your role as a journalist and how should you be informing society's opinion about politics?

NK: I consider myself an activist journalist. I identify myself primarily as an activist, as someone who is driven by my desire for social change. But I happen to actually not like crowds very much. There are a lot of different ways of being an activist. We have this idea in our head that activist equals someone who marches in a rowdy crowd, holds a placard, and screams into a megaphone; that is an activist. You can be an activist in any profession that you choose. You can be an activist doctor, an activist lawyer, an activist entrepreneur, and an activist journalist. It means that you use your skills and talents in the service of social change. That does not mean that you would never go to a protest. I certainly go to protests and rallies, but I am not a very good chanter.

I am a columnist, which means that my role is to have an opinion and to analyze from a certain perspective. There are people whose job is to be a straight-ahead reporter, and they have to be much more guided by the rules of balance. I do not use the word *objectivity* because I do not believe that anyone is objective. Absolutely, you must be fair and balanced, and you must not be a propagandist. You can be a journalist out of your desire for social justice, but you should refuse to be propagandist in the sense of distorting reality for those political ends. Propaganda does not actually serve those political ends. Besides, the real activist journalists are working at FOX, not *The Nation.* We are timid at *The Nation.* At FOX, they are just gloves off. They are campaigning crusader journalists for their particular worldview.

Question: In *Fences and Windows,* you write of the recurring theme of fences acting as barriers to resources, demonstrations, political policies, and other means of affecting change. When have you personally felt the burden of such a fence blocking you from implementing change? How did you respond to this?

NK: I chose the metaphor of fences because in many countries, the only jobs available are as prison guards or as private security guards protecting the "haves" from the "have-nots." We barely notice it anymore because so many of us have accepted the realities of a widening gap between rich and poor. But that kind of system means that the rich have to be protected from the rage of the poor, from the mobility of the poor, or from the needs of the poor, which is why we have so many fences and walls in our supposedly globalized society. This holds whether at the border, where we are seeing more and more people being deported in handcuffs, or at the neighborhood level, with ever more elaborate alarm systems, especially in cities like São Paulo, New Delhi, or Johannesburg, where you have the sharpest divisions. That was why I used that metaphor.

In terms of whether I, personally, have been affected, part of the reality I'm describing is that people like you and me really are not that affected—we sail through life with an illusion. I just sailed through the U.S.–Canada border this morning. Going to Jordan and Iraq, I will have the impression that globalization is real if I just keep my blinders on. I will have the illusion that we really can enjoy the incredible mobility that technology affords us and not see what an incredible privilege it is and that a huge majority of the world's population are shut out and face fences and barriers wherever they try to move, where we are facing open borders and possibilities.

There are barriers that I choose to face if I go to a protest at a trade summit, for example. The Free Trade Area of the Americas summit was recently in Miami. Certainly we were fenced in there, but that was also a privilege. It is a privilege to choose to confront those barriers. For example, in the months leading up to the FTAA summit in Miami, there was steady police harassment of the people whose lives have been most directly impacted by so-called free trade policies in Florida: migrant Mexican farm workers and Latino garment workers, for example. In the months leading up to the summit, the police told these workers that if they went to these protests to speak out against the loss of jobs and land as a result of free trade, they would be arrested and deported. Even the question of who can go to a demonstration in this country is increasingly being regulated. These preemptive arrests that we are seeing at protests, where people are just scooped up without doing anything, might mean an arrest record for some of you, or probably not even that, but it would mean a deportation for somebody in a more precarious position.

Question: You have written extensively about how America is essentially colonizing Iraq. How can young people make decisions that will affect the nation's economic policies over in Iraq and elsewhere? Since the government seems uninterested in the protests of the left wing, what can we do to be more effective?

NK: I don't think we have tried yet, to be perfectly honest. There were some amazing protests against the war before it started. In February 2003, there were at least ten million people around the world taking to the streets. But I would argue that most liberals, in both the U.S. and the U.K., are focusing primarily on refighting the fight about why we went to war in the first place—trying to prove ourselves right, in other words. Iraq really did not have the weapons of mass destruction. Bush lied. The protesters are basically saying, "We were right; you were wrong." You know what? We were right. But the idea of gloating about that after hundreds of American soldiers and thousands of Iraqis have died is just obscene. The war is ongoing. The spoils of war continue to be divided at an alarming rate with incredible profits. The moral of this story is crime pays. If you are Halliburton, it pays really well. If you are Bechtel, it pays very, very well.

The opponents of this war should be concentrating on finding strategic ways to make crime *not* pay. There need to be campaigns that really target companies that are profiting directly. It is really easy to find out who those companies are. I was at Duke University a little while ago. The company that got a contract worth half a billion dollars—the largest contract of its kind ever awarded—to set up Iraq's local government is actually a private company that was spun off from Duke and the University of North Carolina and North Carolina State University. It is called the Research Triangle Institute. I interviewed the company's vice president, who was in charge of the Iraq project, and he admitted to me that nobody at his company had been to Iraq in years and that they applied for the contract before the war even started. Three firms were given the opportunity to bid on this project, but two of them refused because they had problems with the idea of bringing democracy to a country that was about to be invaded. They were also uncomfortable with the idea that they would be working directly for an occupying power, which is sort of new territory for nonprofit research institutes and NGOs, but that is what is happening. So universities are very much involved in the war and occupation, and that is just one example. There are plenty at other colleges as well; you just have to do some digging.

It is really about following the money. It is a terrible shame that the billions of dollars of U.S. taxpayer money awarded by Congress in the name of rebuilding a war-torn country is actually staying for the most part in the United States and lining people's pockets here in the face of an incredible humanitarian crisis in Iraq. Research institutions are taking contracts that have a built-in profit. They are called cost plus, because their costs are covered plus a guaranteed profit of anywhere between 3 and 7 percent. But that money is money that is not going to buy medications in Iraq or to hospitals or to fix the water system. There need to be campaigns that follow the money and make these specific connections.

Question: In *Fences and Windows,* you describe how the anti-globalization movement is the moral stepchild of globalization. In other words, the same connections fostered by globalization also led to a transfer of information between people in various parts of the world who are opposed to globalization. As an outgrowth of globalization itself, which you describe as perpetuating unequal distributions in wealth and power, to what extent does the anti-globalization campaign reproduce the same imbalance? To what extent is the campaign dominated by Western voices? Finally, as a journalist, how do you try to incorporate the voices of people in regions of the world who are at the other end of the wealth, power, and privilege spectrum?

NK: There is a lot in that question. In some ways I would disagree with the premise of the question, though. I say in the foreword to the book that calling it an anti-globalization movement is a misnomer. There are some people who are against globalization; they think that we should all just stay home and grow our own food. These people exist, but they are a very small minority within what is called the anti-globalization movement.

The vast majority of people who galvanized around these movements were driven by the rise of corporate power and the privatization of life. In fact, in many parts of the world, nobody uses terms like *anti-globalization* to describe these movements. In Latin America, for instance, they are anti-capitalists, or they are reacting to neoliberalism; it is an anti-neoliberal movement. For the past five years, Latin America has rejected these policies in many different ways, stopping privatization everywhere from Bolivia to Mexico and kicking out neoliberal presidents in Argentina, Bolivia, Ecuador, and Brazil. They are not saying we do not want to be part of the global economy; rather, they are rejecting a set of economic policies that they call neoliberalism—the policies of privatization, deregulation, and downsizing. The reason why it is globalization is because these policies are global and they are globally enforced by international institutions like the International Monetary Fund and the World Bank—one size fits all, cookie-cutter models.

The most famous example of this was when the IMF went into Russia. A journalist got a copy of one of their structural adjustment documents, where they talk about how Russia had to privatize all of their state enterprises and eliminate all import tax. In the middle of the document, the journalist saw that it said South Korea instead of Russia, because they did some kind of search and replace but missed a couple. When I say it is one size fits all, it is literally the same recipe taken from South Korea and imposed on Russia, and now imposed in Iraq. These policies they are using, when they are imposed all at once, are called shock therapy. That is what they called it in the former Soviet Union, and that is what they are calling it in Iraq. But it is shock therapy imposed through shock and awe in military form. Do not ask permission; just bomb, then take.

It is a willful act to refuse to use the word *globalization* in a movement that is actually rejecting neoliberalism or what the French call "savage capitalism." It is a response to global economic policy, not globalization. It is not the fact of being global that is the problem; it is the policies that are the problem and the fact that they are globally enforced. So people started to respond not just with nationalist solutions but also with international social forums like the one in Porto Alegre, Brazil, where people come together and talk about international strategies to respond to these global policies. Of course we have to be global because they are global, but I do not see that as an irony.

Many said this movement was born in November 1999 on the streets of Seattle. In fact, there had been huge demonstrations of tens of thousands of people in Malaysia, in the Philippines, in India, and they were responding to the exact same policies. There was also the Zapatista uprising in Chiapas, Mexico, on

January 1st, 1994, the day that NAFTA became law, which was also very clearly a response to these same policies. But the World Social Forum, which is the largest gathering of this thing that people call the anti-globalization movement, had its first three meetings in Brazil, and its fourth happened in India. I think this has been part of a concerted effort to fix some of those misconceptions about this being a North American or European movement.

Question: Do you think that your status as a Canadian citizen has allowed you to take a more objective view in evaluating the role of the American government abroad?

NK: I do not know that being a Canadian helps to see what the U.S. is doing on the world stage so much, but I think it does help culturally. Canadians are good watchers. That has to do with the simple fact that we live next to the largest and most powerful country in the world, across the largest undefended border, which is getting more defended by the day. In Canada, we see you, but you don't see us. The experience of seeing everything that is going on but not being seen, not being a part of it because we are next to the largest one-way mirror in the world, this experience makes us more acute observers, whether that is translated into comedy, satire, or media criticism. We are a nation of critics; I don't know if that is good or not.

It is an interesting moment in Canada because since September 11th, the polls show that there is a greater gap between the way Canadians see themselves and the way they see Americans. Before, there was a sense of slow continental integration, a sense that the border was becoming merely a technicality. That has really changed in the past three years because of the rise of militarism and nationalism in the U.S., which Canadians just cannot relate to. It is not so much that Canadians have changed, but I would say that Americans have changed and we do not relate to you as much anymore as we did before. For us Canadians, it is a challenge, because we have to ask ourselves, if we are not that, what are we? We have not answered that yet.

3. DIVERSITY AND EQUALITY
Balancing the Scales

LANI GUINIER, legal scholar

Lani Guinier is the first black woman to become a tenured professor at Harvard Law School. Prior to that appointment, she taught at the University of Pennsylvania Law School and served as head of the voting rights project at the NAACP Legal Defense Fund. Guinier was also a civil rights attorney for more than ten years, and during the Carter administration she served in the Civil Rights Division as special assistant to then–assistant attorney general Drew S. Days. She is the coauthor, with Gerald Torres, of The Miner's Canary: Enlisting Race, Resisting Power, Transforming Democracy. *In this interview, Guinier reminds us that standardized tests more accurately predict the kind of car a student's parents drive than what grades that student will earn during the first year of college. Using race as a diagnostic tool, she teaches about the "miner's canary" and encourages us to enlarge our vision of what democracy means, of what the women's movement might be, and of the mission of higher education.*

Question: In light of the women's movement's historical blindness on issues of race and class, would you share your vision of what you would like to see the women's movement in the United States doing today and how it should interact with international women's groups?

Lani Guinier: Kimberly Crenshaw, a black woman professor who teaches both at UCLA and Columbia, has written an important article on issues of intersectionality, in which she talks about the relationship of white women to people of color, to race. One of her points is that we need to think about race and we need to think about gender each as coalitions in and of themselves. That is, the women's movement needs to be reconceptualized as a coalition of people who are committed to issues of equity in terms of gender. When you think of the women's movement as itself a coalition, it is not just based on an essential identity named Woman, because when you think about Woman, most people, at least in the United States, think about white women, they think about white upper-middle-class women, and then that becomes the defining paradigm for the movement. But if you think about the movement as itself being grounded in the notion of coalition, then the question is, Who are these white upper-middle-class women in coalition with, and what are they in coalition to do? The same thing is true with race. When you think about race and about the black community, you should think about the black community as a coalition between black women and black men. That is a way of both understanding the important elements of a community while also keeping in mind that you create a coalition in order to do something—in order to serve or promote a vision. So it is not just based on who you are, but what you do. I think that using this idea of coalition would be an interesting way of reconceptualizing the women's movement.

My experience is that the group that is most associated with the women's movement, meaning upper-middle-class white women, in some ways has been paralyzed in terms of how to conceptualize the future of this movement. If you take, for example, many women at Harvard Law School, they do not want to talk about gender at all. They do not want to talk about gender because they are afraid that when you speak of gender, you are confirming stereotypes. They have assumed that there is no relevant difference between men and women—that is the way they have been taught, socialized to think about these issues—and yet men still outperform women in law school and in making partner, and women are still underrepresented on the faculty.

There was an interesting book, about fifteen years ago, about women as prisoners of men's dreams, meaning that the women's movement is seeking to obtain what men have, as if what men have is the ultimate ideal, as opposed to suggesting that men could also learn from the experience of women. The goal is to reconceptualize the ideal society not in the image of men, not in the image of women, but in the image of all of the members of this coalition. It requires that you denaturalize some of the assumptions as to what success is, what merit is, what privilege is, which have been, in my opinion, gendered male—certainly at the law school—and begin to question what it means to have success. Many women at law school now determine their own position vis-à-vis success as, Are they doing as well as the men? As opposed to, Is anybody in law school doing what it takes to become a good lawyer in the twenty-first century? Are we teaching all of our students to become public and private problem solvers?

We have a situation at the Harvard Law School where we use as the dominant pedagogy—although it is not as uniform as it once was—a method that was invented over a hundred years ago by Christopher Columbus Langdell. Just as many people would argue that Christopher Columbus did not discover America, I would argue that Christopher Columbus Langdell did not discover the only way to teach the law. Yet we continue to use a method that was adopted in the late 1800s for reasons that may have made sense then when you had a homogenous group of potential practitioners, but in a multiracial, multiethnic community, it may not be the best way for all students to learn. It may not be the best way for students to learn how to practice law when most lawyers no longer go to court and most lawyers do not practice in solo practices. At the time when Christopher Columbus Langdell was discovering his method, most lawyers were litigators, so it made sense to model the litigation paradigm in the classroom. But negotiation/transactional work is much more important in some ways to what a lawyer actually does, yet we are not training lawyers to do that.

Going back to your question, many women feel that rather than questioning the dominant paradigm, they just have to succeed within it. It is what we call in *The Miner's Canary* "climbing backwards up the cheese grater"—repopulating the hierarchy by trying to make it to the top. If you have ever grated cheese on a cheese grater, you will know that what is left in your hand after you have been grating is a bare nubbin of what you used to have. Oftentimes, when you climb backwards up that cheese grater, you are grating off all the things that motivated you to want to succeed in the first place, and who you are becomes indistinguishable from the people that you are presumably trying to replace.

Question: If you were invited to make a speech before the Supreme Court with respect to its deliberations on affirmative action, how would you either defend or reject the policy? What are your objections to and points of agreement with the alternative offered by its opponents, basing admissions not on racial diversity but on economic diversity?

LG: It would be an unusual opportunity to make a speech before the Supreme Court. Most of the time when lawyers argue before the court, they barely get one or two sentences out of their mouths before the Justices interrupt. So assuming I had permission to speak at length for thirty or forty-five minutes without interruption, I would try to get the court to focus first on what the public mission of higher education is in this country. When we think about affirmative action, we tend to start the conversation talking about admissions to institutions of higher education. At least, it is in that context that the issue is before the court right now in terms of the University of Michigan college and law school cases. We treat the issue as if it is simply a matter of who should be admitted to these selective institutions. That is starting the conversation in the wrong place. The conversation needs to start with the mission of these institutions, and then, once you have an understanding of that mission, you can strategize back to understand what admissions policies are appropriate to promote the mission of higher education. The conversation about affirmative action should not take place simply as a question of admission linking it to mission, but it should also be a conversation that opens up questions about institutional practice, because that, too, should be a function of the mission of the institution.

Just as an aside, speaking in terms of the Michigan case, which was argued on April 1, 2003, there were briefs filed as friends of the court by a number of ex-generals and former heads of the military academy, which are now called the military brief, and then there were briefs filed again as friends of the court by some of the Fortune 500 companies. What was interesting is that both the military and the business briefs did exactly what I am proposing—that is, they started with their mission. The military started with its mission of protecting the country's national security and then concluded that having an admission policy that enabled them to recruit a diverse set of potential leaders was essential to their mission, because the legitimacy of the institution depended upon having diversity throughout the ranks in order to avoid some of the fragmentation and communication bottlenecks that occurred during the Vietnam War, when there was a predominantly black and Latino group of soldiers and then virtually all-white officers commanding the forces. There was a disconnect between who was fighting the war and who was making decisions or leadership judgments, and that undermined military effectiveness. Therefore, when the former generals talked about affirmative action, it was clearly linked to the mission of the organization. Business followed the same progression. Now we could take issue with what the business community or even the military were articulating as their mission, but at least they were starting by talking about mission.

When we talk about affirmative action in the context of higher education, instead of talking about the mission of higher education, we talk about what is fair to individuals who have applied to institutions of higher education. We do not talk about the fact that most institutions of higher education have a public, democratic mission. Obviously, Michigan, which is a public institution subsidized by all of the taxpayers, has a public, democratic mission since it is a public school. But even private schools have public missions, because, first of all, education is an essential part of a democracy. In a democracy, we depend on the capacity of citizens to deliberate, to participate, to be involved in decision making; in order to do that, the assumption is that people need to be educated. But in addition, institutions of higher education, even private institutions, are networking opportunities for potential leaders—they are gatekeepers. This also relates to the question of democracy because the assumption is that you need to have a representative group of leaders in order to have a legitimate democracy.

Now, if we had that conversation, and we concluded that having democratic diversity was critical to the mission of higher education, we could have a very different kind of conversation about the kinds of admission protocol that would be appropriate to promote that democratic mission. In my view, that kind of democratic mission requires diversity, not just racial diversity but also socioeconomic diversity. The problem I have with the present framing in which we are either for or against affirmative action is that conversation is taking place almost exclusively on the margins. For example, the majority of people who are getting admitted are not at the center of the conversation, and they should be. There was a recent study by Tony Carnevale, a vice president of the Educational Testing Service, who found that of the 146 most selective colleges and universities in this country, 74 percent of the students come from the richest socioeconomic demographic. That is, 74 percent of the students at the 146 most selective colleges and universities are in the top 25 percent of the income distribution. Only 3 percent of all the students at those schools are in the bottom 25 percent. If you add together the bottom two quartiles, then you have only 10 percent of the students at the 146 most selective colleges and universities. There is a tremendous—what Carnevale calls—"machine of inequality" that is at work that should be at the forefront of the conversation. A small group of very affluent students dominate admission. Assuming that higher education has a democratic mission, why are we practicing democracy, which is supposed to be about all of the people, in a way that allows the elite to dominate these opportunities not only for upward mobility but for potential leadership?

Question: In *The Miner's Canary*, you talk about the need for a fundamental change in the power structures of our society, both cultural and political. What do you think the role of someone such as a white male from a relatively privileged background is in enacting that change, or am I, by nature of my background, my class, my race, and my gender, just part of the problem and powerless as far as what I can do?

LG: One of the concepts that we talk about in *The Miner's Canary* is "political race." The idea of political race starts with the premise that we can learn a lot from those who have been left out and who have been marginalized because of their racial identity. You can make a similar claim in terms of those who have been left out based on gender, based on disability, or based on sexual orientation. That is the whole point of the metaphor of the canary and the mine. The canary was the diagnostic resource for the miners, who would bring this canary into the mines to alert them when the atmosphere was too toxic for the miners. The canary had a more fragile respiratory system, which, when it gave way, was a signal to the miners that there was a problem with the atmosphere in the mines.

The argument that we are making with political race is that the experience of people of color is the experience of the canary. Oftentimes, the way in which we conventionally think about race is that we see things converging around people of color, we see problems that we associate with people of color, and we pathologize the canary. We assume that because this is happening to people of color and we see it, that it must be a problem of those people. The idea of political race is to try to create a sense of connection between the miners and the canary. In fact, your future rests with a better understanding of what is happening to the canary, and you cannot survive—even if you are affluent,

even if you are white, even if you are a male—if you are living in
a toxic environment. In that sense, your liberation is bound up
with the saving of the canary.

So there is a sense in which we start with race as the diagnostic tool. We also start with race because we have seen that those
who have been left out not only have a perspective that others
may not initially appreciate—this is the claim that if you are fish
swimming in water, you may not notice that there is water, and it
is only somebody who is less comfortable in the environment
that may notice there is H_2O. Our argument is that in a culture
that often neglects the importance of community in favor of the
"radical individual," we need to listen to the critique offered by
the canary, and we need to heed the warning signs from those
people who have been left out. These canaries are often the people who have a sense of community, a sense of linked fate, a sense
that they are not alone, because their very survival depends on
being connected to other, similarly situated individuals. Political
race is both a diagnostic tool and a source of solidarity and community, and the goal is to mobilize those two assets to create a
social movement that also brings other people into the movement because it is moving toward a shared vision—not just
fixing the canary, but fixing the atmosphere and the mines.

Let me give you an example of how this has happened in real
life. Before the University of Michigan case raised the stakes on
affirmative action and the use of race in making admissions decisions, the Fifth Circuit ruled that race could not be a factor in
admissions decisions in the 1990s. In response, a group of "canary watchers" at the University of Texas were determined to
ensure that Texas, the flagship school of the University of Texas
at Austin, remained accessible to blacks and Latinos for a num-

ber of reasons related to what I said earlier, but also because the University of Texas had officially discriminated against blacks and Latinos for much of its history. The infamous *Sweatt v. Painter* case came out of the University of Texas. The group of canary watchers understood that blacks and Latinos often did not do as well on the conventional tests that are used to allocate scarce resources in the state's higher education system. There are many more people not only who want to go to UT Austin but who could do the work at UT Austin. Because of shifts in resources from education to prison, there is less money available now to fund public education to meet the demand. You have more and more people who want to go to college, and you have fewer seats.

In order to distribute these scarce resources, these scarce slots, efficiently, meaning without putting a lot of resources into the administration of the admissions program, schools like the University of Texas, the University of Michigan, even Harvard, which could put the resources in if it wanted, rely on the SAT, the LSAT, the GRE, the MCAT, to do a lot of the sorting for them. You might say that makes sense, because these tests are a good measure of merit; they are going to tell us who is going to do well not only at the school but also in the future. That is not, in fact, correct. The "canary watchers" in Texas discovered that the tests are actually a pretty poor predictor of what you are going to do in life and not much better in predicting how well you are going to do your first year in college.

In fact, Harvard did a study of three classes of its graduates over a thirty-year period and found that two things predict success as Harvard measures it. When they were doing this study—I am guessing now; I do not know this to be a fact—I assume that they were looking to see who made a lot of money, who had a lot of fun making the money, and who was giving the money back to the school. Those were their measures of success. How much money do you make? How much do you enjoy your career? Have you become a leader in your community to the point where you now want to include your college in your charitable donations? Two things correlated with success as Harvard defined it: low SAT scores and a blue-collar background. The conclusion seemed to be that if you are given the opportunity to go to a prestigious university, and you are motivated to take advantage of that opportunity, you may in fact better use that opportunity than those people who feel entitled to be there.

Michigan found that in a thirty-year sample of its law school graduates, those with the highest entry-level credentials were no more likely to do well financially. During one period, 1980 to 1989, those with the highest entry-level credentials were among those who did not enjoy their career. That is, if you had high entry-level credentials, you were certainly no more likely to have job satisfaction. Significantly, those with the highest entry-level credentials were among those who were least likely to contribute to the community after they graduated. They were the least likely to mentor younger attorneys, to do public service, to do pro-bono work, or to become leaders in their community— to give back, in other words, to the community that subsidized their education in the first place. One of the hypotheses of the authors of the Michigan study is that the testing regime—what I call the testocracy—undermines people's understanding of why they are coming to an institution of higher education. It communicates the wrong message. It tells people that you deserve to be here, and therefore you have no obligation to give back to anybody. You are here to do well but not necessarily to do good.

The canary watchers at Texas who were looking at all of this data—and similar data was also true at Texas—found that at the college level in particular, these tests, which are not predicting performance long-term, actually do correlate with something. Peter Sacks has recently clarified what that something is. These tests allow you to predict what kind of car someone's parents drive. He calls it the "Volvo effect." If you know someone's test score, you are better able to predict their parents' wealth than you are to predict their first-year college grades. With Michelle Fine and Jane Balin, I did a study at the University of Pennsylvania Law School, where we got all of the LSAT scores of all of the students over a four-year period, and we found that if you knew someone's LSAT, you could predict their first-year law-school grades 14 percent of the time, which means that 86 percent of the time, you would be wrong. Nationwide, the LSAT is 9 percent better than random in predicting law-school grades. Yet there is a stronger relationship between SAT scores and grandparent wealth than between SAT or LSAT scores and first-year grades. Because of this correlation with affluence rather than aptitude, you have the situation I referred to before where 74 percent of the seats at these highly selective institutions are going to the richest 25 percent of people in the United States.

In Texas the canary watchers were using race as a diagnostic tool. They understood that people of color were not doing as well on these tests, and they were concerned about the fact that if you just relied on these tests, without considering race, they would have a predominantly white institution in a state that is becoming increasingly people of color. They then looked to see which high schools were feeding into the selective college, their flag-ship school. There are approximately fifteen hundred high schools in Texas, and one hundred fifty of those schools were providing almost 75 percent of the freshman students. Ten per-cent of the high schools of Texas dominated access to this public institution that was subsidized by all of the taxpayers of the state. That 10 percent, those high schools, were from suburban Dallas, suburban Houston, suburban Austin. They then found that grades in high school are the best predictor of grades in col-lege—if that is all you are interested in. I happen to think that that is a thin measure, what Carnevale calls "skinny merit," when you use just one idea, one concept, one test, to determine merit. But if you are only going to use one thing, then grades in high school are a better predictor of your college success than your SAT scores. They came up with the idea of creating the op-portunity for people in the top 10 percent of any high school throughout the state to attend the flagship school. So if you were in the top 10 percent of a high school from San Antonio or in the top 10 percent of a high school in a depressed area of Houston, you would still be automatically eligible for admission to the University of Texas at Austin.

They put this bill before the Texas legislature. They started with race as their diagnostic tool, but by the time they got to the Texas legislature, they needed allies. They were looking for coalition partners. (Not all of the people, by the way, who were involved in the initial research were black or Latino. At the time, the head of the Mexican American Legal Defense Fund in Texas, Al Kaufman, was a white male.) When they got this bill before the Texas legislature, it passed by one vote. That one vote was cast by a white Republican conservative legislator who rep-

resented a district in rural west Texas. He voted for the 10 percent plan because the canary watchers were able to show him
that under the "testocracy," not a single one of his constituents
had been admitted to the University of Texas for many of the
previous ten years. They built a coalition between blacks and
Latinos who were being excluded and working-class and poor
rural whites who were being excluded by an admissions regime
that was preferring affluence to a more robust notion of merit.

The 10 percent plan has been in effect now for what will
be five years in June [2003]. Fifty percent of the class at the University of Texas at Austin comes in through the 10 percent plan.
Fifty percent of the class still comes in based on SAT scores,
teacher recommendations, and the same kinds of things that you
think got you into Harvard. Of the students who come in pur-
suant to the 10 percent plan, whether they went to a resource-
starved school or a very well-endowed school, whether they are
white, black, Latino, or Asian, if they come in under the 10 percent plan, they have a higher freshman GPA at the University of
Texas at Austin than those students who are still coming in under the "testocracy." The ten-percenters, in other words, are out-
performing in college those students who are coming in under
conventional credentials. The students with the highest persistence rate, students who not only come in as freshmen but who
then return as sophomores, are black women.

The point is that you start with race because it is a diagnostic
tool; you start with race because people of color who have been
left out are often those most committed to collective action to
make a change. But you use that commitment to collective
struggle to create a vision that others can follow. That is what has
happened in Texas, because the 10 percent plan has opened up

opportunity. It is not as carefully targeted to blacks as affirmative action was. That is, the percentage of blacks now at the University of Texas at Austin is about 3.8 percent; when they used affirmative action, it was 4 percent. The percentage of Mexican Americans, however, is higher. The percentage of working-class whites is higher still. I am not saying that the 10 percent plan is a panacea; I am not saying that it is a substitute for affirmative action; but I am saying that it is a more transformative way of understanding the role of affirmative action. Thinking experimentally about admission in the context of mission, keeping the democratic mission of public institutions in mind, and watching the canary can open up opportunity for the miners as well. The story of the Texas 10 percent plan shows that it does not so much matter what your personal race or identification is but whether you link your fate with people of color who have been left out.

Question: In *The Tyranny of the Majority,* you have described proportional representation as opposed to winner-take-all representation, which limits the diversity of factions within legislative bodies. Instead of the way that current decisions are made by members of the UN, do you have a vision for some form of proportional representation on a global level? If so, could you explain that vision more concretely?

LG: I am not on a crusade to get either the United Nations or all of the countries of the world to adopt a particular form of voting, which is what proportional representation is basically about. For those who haven't read *The Tyranny of the Majority,* you may not know that there is something called proportional representation, and it has nothing to do with quotas. Most of the world's democracies, in fact, practice proportional representation as a way of aggregating votes to determine who is going to be part of a collective decision-making body—in the United States it would be the equivalent of our Congress; in other countries, it is the national assembly. In our country, we use what the questioner referred to as winner-take-all, single-member districts. That is, our voters get to choose who is going to represent them in the national, collective decision-making body by choosing between candidates who run for office from a geographically defined area. Whoever wins the most votes within that geographically defined area, which is called a district, is the winner. That means if you get 51 percent of the votes in this geographically defined district, you win *all* of the power to represent all of the voters within that district. What about the 49 percent who voted against you? You get to represent them too. In my view that is not democratic, because I think people should be represented by people they voted *for*, not by people they voted against. That is number one.

Number two: who gets to draw those districts? Do the voters get to draw the districts which determine where they are going to exercise their franchise? No, the voters are placed in these geographically defined districts by incumbent politicians who draw the districts with one thing in mind, and it has very little to do with democracy. It has to do with their own reelection. The incumbents draw districts around groups of voters who they presume will vote for them. In fact, in the election in 2002, within a month before the election, it was pretty clear what the outcome would be of probably 80 to 90 percent of the congressional races, because the incumbents, with the aid of computers, are so successful in designing these districts that they can determine in advance who is going to vote for them, who is going to vote against them. They have access to all kinds of demographic information about the voters, and they cluster people so that they waste the votes of those who are going to vote against them, meaning that they put just enough people who are their opponents in the district so that they can meet one-person, one-vote requirements, meaning that they have the right number of people in the district. But that group, who are essentially wasting their vote, meaning that they are voting but their vote is not influencing the outcome, are called filler people—they fill up the population demographics, but they do not have much influence.

The voters know this. Therefore you see declining levels of turnout when people realize that essentially the election has already taken place even before Election Day. In other words, the districting process, which is controlled by the incumbent politicians, is the "real" election. Then in November, we have a ritual in which people go to vote, but in fact, in most cases, the election outcome has already been decided. In the election in 2002, there were in the beginning maybe thirty—out of the more than four hundred congressional districts that were presumably up for election—only thirty were even competitive. Then, as it got closer to the election, there were only ten or twelve that had outcomes that were unknown. Indeed, during the period of 1991 to 2001, there were less than a handful of districts around the entire country—so we are talking elections in 1992, 1994, 1996, 1998, and 2000—in those five election cycles, there were only a total of five or six congressional districts which changed hands from one party to the other more than once during that cycle. Essentially, our system fixes the outcome by giving control to the politicians rather than giving choice to the voters.

Proportional representation reverses that. Proportional representation says that politicians are only elected in proportion to the percentage of votes that they actually receive. For example, when South Africa became an all-race democracy, the African National Congress (ANC) polled about 64 percent of the votes in the national election, and members of the ANC then occupied about 65 percent of the seats in the national assembly. The Inkatha Freedom Party polled about 11 percent of the votes and got about 11 percent of the seats in the national assembly, and then the white Afrikaners polled about 17 or 18 percent of the votes and got about 18 percent of the seats in the national assembly. So proportional representation basically creates motivation for the politicians to mobilize voters because they only get to sit in the national assembly to the extent that they get people out to the polls to support them. The politicians are not in control in the same way that they are in the United States' winner-take-all system. Our system, not surprisingly, is a vestige of British rule. The only countries in the world that still use winner-take-all, single-member districts were all former colonies of Great Britain.

What is interesting is if you look at countries like Germany, which has a mixed system—that is, it uses some single-member districts and some proportional voting—they have much higher levels of satisfaction among the population with the democracy, and they also have much higher levels of turnout, *and* they have much higher levels of turnout among poor people and working-class people. In our country, about half of the people who could vote do not vote, and among those who do not vote, a disproportionate number are making less than twenty-five thousand dollars a year, whereas in Europe the disparity between those who vote and those who do not based on income is more like 5 percent. So I think proportional representation is a good idea. On the other hand, I do not believe that democracy is simply about voting or elections. That goes back to the point I was making earlier that education and training people to become leaders in a civic sense—not just in the sense of becoming an elected official, but becoming a leader and active participant in their community—is just as important an element of having a robust democracy, and that is why I think we have to enlarge our view of what democracy means, not only in the context of elections, but also in the context of the discussion of affirmative action.

Question: Why do Americans remember the Salem witch trials so readily, yet few people know of King Philip's War, in which hundreds of American Indians were killed? The witch trials seemed to evaluate an issue of sex and gender discrimination that is much more easily discussed over issues of race discrimination. Do you feel that this is a distinction that is occurring in society today? How does this compare to gender discrimination?

LG: We have a tendency in this society to compare apples and oranges. One way to compare apples and oranges is to say they are both fruit. One way is to move up to the larger category, and you could say that both race and gender are categories of identity, and therefore they might have much in common. But when you get down to the specifics of the apples and oranges, you will see that in our society gender is not a line around which people are physically segregated. People do not lead gendered lives in the same way that they live socially isolated lives vis-à-vis race. Ironically, the group that is most socially isolated in terms of race is affluent whites. Those of you who are here at Harvard, if you are white, are more likely to have gone to a high school in which whites were not only a majority but an overwhelming majority

of the student body. Given studies at other schools, it is the people of color who have more friends who are of a different race
than the white people.

Indeed, in one of my classes, we did an exercise in which we
went around the room and asked people, "What does it take to
survive at Harvard Law School? What does it take to succeed at
Harvard Law School and in the legal profession?" What was interesting was that women of color, in particular a small group of
black women, said that in order for their group to succeed, they
had to demonstrate that they were capable of fraternizing with
everybody. They had to demonstrate their cultural competency
with all cultures. They had to show that they were not just talking with each other but were in fact in dialogue with everybody
at the institution in order to demonstrate that they could succeed, whereas for the white students that was not an element of
success. A white person could succeed in the institution without
ever talking to a student of color. It is both that segregation, that
sense of social isolation, and the fact that one group has the burden of attempting to interact with the other that makes gender
so different than race. In terms of gender, you could say that a
white male could succeed without ever talking to a woman, but
because women are almost half the student body in the law
school, that would be difficult.

If you look at some of the research on women—talking about
women as women—the research on women suggests that especially affluent women are more likely to internalize failure, to
blame themselves as the source of a problem rather than understand that the problem may be structural and may be affecting
many other people. A really silly anecdote: a razor company was
testing its razors and was doing an experiment in which they had

given out defective razors, and they were observing the way in which men and women used these razors through a one-way mirror. They noticed that the men, when they were shaving and had a defective razor, would look at the razor and say, "This razor is defective," and throw it away. The women, when they were using the defective razors, would begin to wring their hands; they believed they were cutting themselves because there was something wrong with their technique. That is this idea of internalizing failure rather than looking beyond yourself to the larger social circumstances. That is an anecdotal example of a larger phenomenon that does not define all women and does not define all men, but there is at least a significant population in which that becomes descriptive of a reality. If you felt greater solidarity with other people who were similarly situated—if that is the whole point of the women's movement, of consciousness-raising, of sharing stories—you would begin to think, "Hey, I am not alone. This is not about me. This is about not only we, but we moving together, to make change for everyone."

KATHA POLLITT, writer

Katha Pollitt's literary career began when she was in the fourth grade and composing poetry in her bedroom. Her political savvy developed as she debated Stalin's policies with her parents over the dinner table. Though she has received both NEA and Guggenheim fellowships for her poetry, she is perhaps best known for her incisive analyses of politics, popular culture, and gender. Pollitt's books include Reasonable Creatures: Essays on Women and Feminism, Subject to Debate: Sense and Dissents on Women, Politics, and Culture, *and* Antarctic Traveller, *a book of poetry. She has written for* The Nation *since 1980. In her interview, Pollitt reviews the advances feminism has made thus far and debunks antifeminist writers, exploring options for contemporary women and men negotiating both career and family.*

Question: Could you tell us about how you became a writer and social critic?

Katha Pollitt: I always wanted to be a writer. I started writing poetry when I was in fourth grade. The way my daughter rides horses, I wrote poetry. I would come home, I would go up to my room, I would sit on my bed, and I would scribble away. As for social criticism, I grew up in a very left-wing household, so those ideas were very much a part of the dinner table conversation and the endless debate over Stalin that went on every night. All that just sank in.

I grew up in the Old Left, basically. When I went to college, there was the New Left: antiwar demonstrations, student strikes. I was in the unusual position that my parents approved of what I was doing. They thought it was great. When we took over university buildings and all got arrested, by the time we came back there were flowers from my parents. It was all wonderful to them, so it was sort of hard to rebel.

Those two tracks of writing and politics were always there for me. They do not always come together in my writing. For example, my poetry is not so political, or, I flatter myself, it is political in a more subtle way. It is there, but not on the surface as it is in my political column. But I feel I am still bringing them together; it is not a finished process.

Question: In reference to your article "Backlash Babies," could you elaborate on what sort of changes you would like to see occurring in the workplace so that women have the ability to have children if they choose while pursuing their career?

KP: "Backlash Babies" was a response to *Creating a Life* by Sylvia Ann Hewlett, an economist who has been writing since the Flood about how feminism and the women's movement have done no good at all to women in their capacity as mothers. This book, which was called *Baby Hunger* in Britain (that was too much for the American audience), argued that women think they have all the time in the world to get married, but they don't. That is theme number one: you think you have all the time in the world to have babies but you really do not. She has very scary statistics about infertility. This book was couched as, Isn't this terrible? There was a little piece of it that was about trying to think of ways society could be more friendly to the life project of marriage and family. She was in favor of parental leave, being able to arrange your work hours differently, and flextime; you know, the whole laundry list making jobs less of an hour cage for the worker. But the reason why this book got an enormous amount of media attention is that basically it was saying to women, if you want to get married and have a family, you have to spend your twenties hunting a husband. You have to be "intentional" about it. She felt that young women today work, work, work, look up, and it is too late. You have to arrange a life so that you will have plenty of time for this intentional search for your mate. Then, when you find this mate, you should have children right away because your fertility has probably already declined. Only a few eggs left; you better scramble them right away.

There were a couple of interesting things about this book. One is that most of the supposed facts are not, in fact, factual. She starts off saying that only 51 percent of high-achieving women have children—she defines "high-achieving" in terms of income—so there are problems there already. Only 51 percent manage to have children, even though only 14 percent said in college that they did not want to have children. This is like a barn door to walk through! How many things did I say I wanted to do when I was in college that I did not do? I changed my mind; life got in the way; things happened. The idea that if you said you wanted to have children when you were twenty and when you are forty you do not have those children, that this is the source—as for her it inevitably was—of tremendous despair and mourning, just does not accord with the experience of many women who do not have children who, when they were in their teens, thought they would. Here is another interesting point: Sylvia Ann Hewlett has five children, and she had the last one when she was fifty-one, so she is a walking advertisement against her own thesis. This is true of all the antifeminist writers, actually: they do not live the life they are prescribing for other people. For one thing, they are not stay-at-home mothers like they think everyone ought to be. They are writers, just like me. I stay home; my office is at home. It is not like I am cooking all day, and neither are they. (I am e-mailing my friends all day.)

Danielle Crittenden is another one. She wrote a book called *What Our Mothers Didn't Tell Us,* which is that we have to get married by the time we are twenty-three. We have to have our babies right away, then we look around and see what we can do. Well, so her mother did not tell her that. Both she and Sylvia Ann Hewlett believe—now you've got me going—that at bottom, you have to be the deferential person in the marriage. Your husband is following his clear-blue-sky trajectory and you are fitting your life in around that, and if you don't do that, then you cannot have a marriage. One thing that Danielle Crittenden especially made fun of was women who kept their names upon getting married. Well, guess who kept her name upon getting married? Danielle Crittenden, who is married to David Frum, the former speechwriter of George W. Bush. She is not Danielle Frum. As for being a stay-at-home mom, please! She has a housekeeper, a cook, and a nanny. When you know a little bit about who these people are and what their real lives are like, you have to wonder what they think they are doing. Why is it good for them but not for you? At least they should say, "Look, it has worked out for me, maybe it will work out for you. Give it a try."

All this is not to say that there is not a whole lot of work that needs to be done around all these issues for both sexes of combining family and work and maybe a little fun, too, in our lives. But the solution is not to spend your twenties looking for a man.

Question: What practical suggestions do you have then for both women and men today who are caught in the dilemma of career versus family?

KP: I have had such a weird life that I don't think I have very good advice for people who follow that straight and narrow corporate path. I would say things like, "Think of something else to do. Don't take a job where you have to work ninety hours a week doing something that you don't really love. Don't find yourself saying, 'I don't get to see my children grow up because I'm so busy making money for the boss.' Rethink that project."

I would also say there needs to be a social movement to change the workplace. These are not problems that can be readily solved at the individual level; right now there are certain kinds of work that are very hard to do in a part-time way. For example, it is very hard to be a part-time lawyer. There are women who live in my building who have had children and they are staying home with the kids, and I would say, "Why can't they do part-time law?" Well, the law does not lend itself to doing it in a part-time way—at least that is what I was told. If you do take one of these tracks specially designed for women, you never make partner, but you get to work fewer hours. But people who work part-time work a lot more than they are paid for because of the creep of the work that needs to be done.

The essential thing is that the husband and wife, if we are speaking of a heterosexual married couple (how old-fashioned), have a sense that this is going to be a problem for both of them, not just for her. Maybe the fact that one person makes more money than the other does not mean that the person who makes less money gets to have no career at all. In conventional arrangements, a relationship starts out very equal, then as it becomes more domestic and children are added to the mix, you turn around and think, "I am doing all the housework. I am doing all the cooking. We're moving because my husband got a job.

Uh-oh. There's no work for me in it, and I don't know anybody there. I'm miserable and I'm taking tranquilizers." I know women who have ended up like this. So you want to have it be seen as a problem for both people and not a problem for just the woman. One thing that is wrong with most books about family-life balance is that they see it as the woman's problem. The man is not going to have to change. The woman is going to have to juggle and finagle. If you start out from that position, I don't think you are going to end up in the place where you want to be.

Question: In "In the Waiting Room," you discuss how young women today are more likely to oppose legal abortion than their mothers. To what would you attribute this shift: effective, reactionary propaganda or, perhaps, some kind of rebellion where kids these days reject the values of their more liberal parents? Is this part of a larger trend? Are neoconservatives the hippies of our generation?

KP: I would like to make one qualification regarding that piece, which is about poor women who needed money for their second-trimester abortions. I cite a *New York Times* story that claims young women are less likely to be pro-choice than their mothers. The article was suggestive, but it was still just anecdotal. The author interviews two people in Minnesota and decides she's found a trend. When you read a "trend story," you need to look carefully at the evidence it presents, because you can make a trend out of nothing. You can make a trend out of interviewing three people in a coffee shop. You find a study over here, a childhood memory over there. You put it all together, and supposedly you have described something that is happening. Stories like that are worthless. The editor of that piece might just as well have said, "I know some young girls and, gosh, they think nothing of having an abortion," which is the other trend story about abortion and the young. Let's write an article about how young women today are even more pro-choice than their mothers. You could find evidence for that, too. I am not sure that young women today are, in fact, less pro-choice.

The word *feminist* is hard for many women to claim even though, if you ask them "Are you in favor of economic equality? Are you in favor of social equality? Are you in favor of equality in the home?"—you could name everything that feminism is about and they would say, "Yes, yes, yes."

"So are you a feminist?"

"No."

That is because that word for them is identified with man hating, being a lesbian, not shaving your legs. Similarly, pro-choice has successfully been cast as the frivolous, cruel, baby-killing, hard-line position. If we spoke of "anti-choice," it would be a little more obvious what was at stake, but "pro-life," well we all want to be pro-life. Young women are still having abortions at high rates, and the freedom to have a legal abortion is the bottom line of pro-choice. But it is also true that in many parts of the country, there is a Christian-conservative religious revival going on. There is abstinence education in the schools where the kids are filled with nonsense about abortion and its consequences. People are subject to a constant barrage of anti-choice propaganda, from the White House on down. It is not so surprising that this has some effect.

Are the neoconservatives the hippies of today? There may be something to that. My daughter, who is in tenth grade, won't come on a demonstration with me. In fact, when I went to the last big peace demonstration in New York, she went shopping with her friend Kate and came home with a pair of genuine camouflage pants from an army-navy store. She said, "I feel a little weird now that I know they were actually worn by a real soldier." I've been making fun of camouflage as a fashion statement ever since she could remember, so there was a message in that for me. If you grow up with liberal, progressive, feminist values, then you may express your individuality by questioning them. You have to fight with your parents about something. For me it was Stalin. For you people it is something else.

Question: You are a strong advocate of equal women's rights across the globe, saying that certain human rights are fundamentally morally right and claiming that they are the root of many social and economic problems. However, many people are reluctant to presumptuously impose their own values on other cultures. What do you see as the right balance between respecting another culture's values and ensuring women's human rights?

KP: That is a tough question that can be answered on many levels. In the real practical world, walking into another culture with all your fine ideas probably won't get you very far any more than it would get an Islamic fundamentalist very far if he showed up in this class and tried to persuade you to live a life according to those precepts. Culture is not a single thing. Think of our own culture. It has aspects that are retrograde, violent, and callous and aspects that are humanistic, humane, and generous. Which is the real America? They are both the real America. I would think that every culture has in it the potential for both oppression and liberation.

There are many different possibilities within each culture, but a Western person, an American person, walking into a foreign culture and telling people how they should live is probably not going to be a very successful project. You have to devote yourself for a long time to living in places and understanding how they work and trying to see what people there need. Maybe for them the veil is not the big issue. Maybe the big issue for them is education, which is what in fact almost any Afghan woman would tell you. They would say, "Forget the veil. That is not the problem. The problem is we do not know how to read. We do not have enough to eat. We do not have any doctors. We cannot live lives that fulfill any of our possibilities."

Question: How do we get feminism to not be perceived as a movement of white upper-class women?

KP: Feminism is always being called white middle class, but I do not know how true that is. There are a lot of black and Latina feminists that reconfigure feminist ideas to suit their own ethnic identities and subcultures. Certainly, feminism has been most successful at moving women into the professions because the big success of feminism in America has been the removal of legal barriers to equality rather than social support for everybody. We do not have that for anybody, male or female. It's sink or swim in this country. Of course, there is still a lot of discrimination, but you can get the qualification, and that makes a big difference.

To some extent, blue-collar women have benefited also. There are more good jobs for working-class women, although most women of whatever class are still working in mostly female job categories. But because the visible successes of feminism are women politicians, women doctors, women lawyers, women engineers, women doing something in a male world, there is an impression that feminism has done little for working-class women. I do not think that is true. Let's take welfare in a historical light. There was a moment when a woman could not get welfare with a man living in her house. The social workers in the 1960s would come to your house at odd hours to see if there was a man there. Unemployed fathers would have to move out in order for the family to get welfare, so welfare broke up families. The feminist critique said that was wrong. It shouldn't be that in order to get welfare you cannot have a sex life, you cannot have a love life, you have to be celibate. That was an effective argument, and it changed the welfare rules. Unfortunately, now we have "welfare reform," where once again needy women and children are deprived of support. It's a continuing struggle.

Question: A lot of people think that there already is equality of rights. The issues that have to be addressed are very hard ones to address with any sort of laws or changes in policy; sometimes they are more embedded than that. What suggestions do you have for people or the movement to change these sorts of things that are more embedded than laws can really work with?

KP: On the surface, our laws do look very equal. But a rule can look neutral on its face but not work out neutrally in practice. For example, the laws related to social security and employment are all written for the male employment pattern, which is continuous unbroken employment. A woman leaves the workforce to care for a sick relative, which our culture more often has women doing. She does not get unemployment because she has not been laid off. "Laid off" means you haven't been fired and you haven't voluntarily left. Because of family responsibilities, women tend to cycle in and out of the workforce. Also, women tend to have the kinds of jobs that disappear, especially poor women. As Barbara Ehrenreich pointed out in *Nickel and Dimed,* nobody works for five years at McDonald's. The job is set up for people to do for just a little while and then leave. They wear you out.

Women, in other words, are much more likely to be in the workplace in a way where they don't get unemployment and they don't build up pension rights because they move around more and go in and out of the workforce. They end up with less social security. So, on the face of it, there is nothing about gender in the law, but it has very gendered consequences.

Pierre Bourdieu, the wonderful French sociologist, makes the point that the law actually does have a big effect on how people live. It shapes not just our ideas about what is normal, but it also influences the structure of work on a very deep level. And that structure influences the choices people make. Before you know it, the gender system of inequality has been reproduced, but it feels to people like choices they have made. That is how society works. You magically want to do the thing that is laid out for you to do.

Feminism is more than a challenge to formal, official discrimination. It is also about how people feel about each other and how they feel about themselves. What kinds of relations are men and women going to have? Those are intimate and personal questions that can make people feel quite threatened. I think that is one reason a woman might not like to identify as a feminist. She might think, "What if I want to get married? What if I get married and I want to change my name?" Isn't that interesting that only women ever seem to say that? How come no man ever says, "I can hardly wait to get married so I can change my name!" At that level, where people feel threatened by change, they do not want to make that deep critique. I have known a lot of people who have not made that deep critique. Sometimes they end up in strange places that do not necessarily make them happy.

Things are different for young people now, and it is probably up to young people themselves to figure out where those fissions are between the equal life we would all like to have and getting there. I am on an e-mail list with a lot of feminists who are even older than I am, and they think nothing has changed. I don't see how people can say that. I think life is quite different for women now than in, say, 1960. But that is another reason why it can feel odd for a young woman to call herself a feminist. It might feel like there is nothing to fuss about. "Everything's great. What's the problem?" By the time you see what the problems are, you are too old to do anything about them. No, no! If young people talk to each other about these issues, they might actually uncover some interesting things.

Question: Do you think that a magazine like *Glamour* or *Seventeen* can, in fact, have positive political empowering messages, or does the overall context wipe them out?

KP: I think you said it yourself. *Glamour,* under Ruth Whitney, the previous editor, always had one or two serious articles about something that was really interesting. My experience writing for *Glamour* was a nightmare, because they made me rewrite everything to fit their idea of their reader, who was not as intelligent as I think their readers are. But still, these were articles about serious things. I won prizes for these articles that did not actually appear in the format in which I had written. The magazines for grown-up women are the same. *Vogue, Elle, Marie Claire.* They all have the occasional piece of real content, and the official message is "Be all that you can be." Except it's "Be all that you can be—have a facelift." Maybe I am being too puritanical. I like clothes; I wear makeup. I even like to cook —a recipe or two. But the relentless focus on appearance is depressing. The notion of beauty is unbelievably narrow and destructive.

You know how it is that the official message is one thing, but the real message is something else? I will give you an example. Let's take eating disorders. I had a graduate student who was very beautiful, slender, and charming. At a certain point, she started talking about the eating disorders that she used to have. This woman had a figure like she had just walked out of the pages of *Seventeen* magazine, but in her past she had had this problem. So what does she do now? She works for the Bulimia Foundation. She goes around to high schools and talks to the girls about the terrors and horrors of eating disorders. But actually, she's a walking advertisement for eating disorders! All a teenage girl would think looking at her is, "Oh, wow! If I make myself throw up enough, maybe I can look like that!" They wouldn't have some two-hundred-pound woman go around to schools saying, "All right, so I am overweight, but the important thing is I'm not bulimic anymore." Instead, they have a really cute girl, so that the official message and the message actually being given are in contradiction to each other.

I think women's magazines are like that. I will just give you one more example, my favorite one. Every single one of the ones for grown-ups has a new diet in it: lose five pounds in five minutes. Lose that last ten pounds so you'll look beautiful in your coffin. If you put a grapefruit on your head, you will lose weight. But every single magazine features recipes that are loaded with calories. On the cover, typically, will be some unbelievably gooey dessert. Anybody who cooks and eats like that is going to have a weight problem. So here again, they make you fat, and then they have to make you thin. Now, if you actually got thin, if diets worked, how many would you need? One. The only way the diet part of the magazine could work is if you didn't do the recipe part. But they want you to do both, so you are on this cycle that keeps you reading the magazine. That's the way it works.

As you can tell, I am quite a student of these magazines, which I do read and even have bought. I'm probably the only person in New York City who has ever read *Family Circle*. But they are not good for you.

Question: Are there any instances in which you think the feminist movement has gone too far for its cause? How can feminists go about spreading their message without alienating many who might share their views but disagree with their methods? For example, those who might want gender equality but associate feminists with bra burning extremists.

KP: There was a very brief moment in American history—it lasted for about three weeks—when feminists, in the rush of euphoria of suddenly being able to see their experience of being a woman in America politically, tried to burn a bra, one bra. The most famous piece of underwear in all of human history was that bra that was not burned but dropped into a trash can at the 1968 Miss America Pageant in Atlantic City. Miss America still goes on with all of her nonsense, but that bra is really history.

I do not think there is a lot of truth to the stereotype that a feminist can't wear pretty clothes, can't care about her appearance, is not interested in sex, love, or men. A lot of people who would call themselves feminists are middle-class married women; they do not fit the stereotype at all. That stereotype is used to say to young women, "If you call yourself a feminist, you are not going to have a boyfriend; you are not going to get married; you are not going to have children. You are just going to be lonely and miserable." That is not true at all.

When confronted with the question, What could feminists be doing differently? I don't know. I mean, look at me. I am wearing pretty earrings. I have two necklaces and these lovely velvet clothes that were rather expensive and black, the fashionable New York color to represent my city when I travel. I dye my hair; I am wearing makeup. What more could I be doing? Assuming there is still something called the feminist movement, which is also a little problematic, I would say it is too tame. It is always trying to say, "Yes, having an abortion is such a terrible, terrible thing. But it should be your choice." When was the last time you heard someone identified with the pro-choice movement, someone from NARAL, someone from the Feminist Majority, someone from the National Organization of Women [NOW] say, "You know, sometimes having an abortion is a really good idea. Sometimes having an abortion can be a way that a woman really does solve a terrible problem. Sometimes it can be a mark of being an adult." If you look at the fifteen-year-old who has the baby and the fifteen-year-old who has the abortion, it is not so clear that the one who has the baby is the one who is doing the mature, responsible thing as opposed to the one who is thinking a little bit about what kind of mother she can be and what kind of life she and that child are going to have. Pro-choice organizations tend not to talk this way; they emphasize the moral pain and agony of this decision in order to say, "This is a serious choice; women are not frivolous." But to me, you have already conceded too much when you have said that. Why is it on the table that to decide whether to have a baby could ever be a frivolous choice? It is never a frivolous choice. You know your life as no one else does; why should you have to demonstrate to the world that you are suffering about it? The feminist movement should become much more radical, and if people are so afraid of it, they should give people something to fear. How about that? I like that. That is such a good sound bite. I know I'll win a lot of friends and influence people with that.

4. *BRUTALITY, BLOODSHED, AND RESOLUTION*

A Violent Inheritance

MARTHA MINOW, legal scholar

Martha Minow's research focus includes equality and inequality, human rights, war crimes and genocide, and pluralism. Minow has taught at Harvard Law School for more than twenty years and has twice served as director for the Harvard University Program on Ethics and the Professions. She is an adviser to Facing History and Ourselves, *an organization that encourages the study of history with an emphasis on political participation and decision making. She is also cochair of an interfamily initiative,* Children's Studies at Harvard, *which promotes interdisciplinary, collaborative research on children and society. Minow has written several books, including* Breaking the Cycles of Hatred: Memory, Law, and Repair *and* Between Vengeance and Forgiveness: Facing History after Genocide and Mass Violence. *Minow explores with us the origins of hateful acts, the path from vengeance to forgiveness, and how to change people's consciousness.*

Question: Could you tell us a bit about your background?

Martha Minow: I am old enough so that the Vietnam War was a framing experience for my consciousness. I was a protester, but I was twelve. That was a very pivotal experience for me. The war ended by the time I went to college at the University of Michigan. People took me around to show me where the protests had been. Then fast-forward, I wrote a book when I was in my early years of teaching called *Making All the Difference* that addresses legal treatment of people who are defined as different by the law, who are marked by race, by gender, by disability, or by religion as being different from the norm. After I wrote the book, I got a phone call from a woman named Margot Strom, who runs an organization called Facing History and Ourselves. She said, "I just want to thank you because we are going to use your materials in our teaching."

I said, "Tell me about what you do."

She said, "We run a program that teaches teachers to teach young people about the Holocaust in an effort to try to prevent future mass atrocities."

When she said that, I thought to myself, "That is really more important than anything I am writing about." Ever since that time, I have been working with them.

Question: If you had to identify the most crucial area or issue that needs to be addressed in order to correct the social origins of hateful acts, what would you choose and why?

MM: Ever since I was twelve, I have sat writing on pieces of paper, "What are the causes of violence and intergroup hatred?" and trying to find where the weak link is in the chain. I haven't found a weak link in the chain. If you find it, let me know. But what I have concluded is that every one of the links is worth tackling, so let me identify one of them.

One is the ability of unscrupulous leaders to use mass media and other techniques to tap into mythologized histories. This certainly happened in Rwanda recently. It happened in Bosnia, it happened in South Africa, and it happened even earlier in Germany. When leaders are interested in mobilizing their own power and authority but do not have a great agenda, they turn to the tactic of creating scapegoats. They do so successfully by tapping into some mythologized versions of the histories of the groups. That is one thing to tackle.

How do you tackle that? One way is by getting richer, more

complicated versions of history into people's consciousness, trying to make sure that young people learn the history of their own countries in ways that are not couched simply in the form of winners and losers, victims and perpetrators. Another is to fight for free speech everywhere because the leaders who have been successful in mobilizing that kind of support have almost invariably had total or large control of the media. A third thing to do is to work from the highest levels of government to the most intimate contexts of family life to battle the tendency to dehumanize any particular group of people.

Question: What is your perspective on hate speech codes? How do you approach the argument that just as with hate crime laws, hate speech codes can cause many unintended consequences, like chilling debate around college campuses?

MM: I do not support hate speech codes. I believe that they do have a danger of killing speech. They have an even greater danger of creating martyrs around the free speech ideal that then distracts attention away from the underlying mistreatment of people through hateful words. There is a kind of foreshortening of the debate around these issues when people are polarized in a form that recapitulates the very problems and dynamics of hatred that people on both sides are trying to change. In the debates over hate speech, people tend to assume that their own position is totally right and that there is no possibility of any truth on the other side. Particularly if these discussions are going on in an academic context, that is incredibly disappointing because we should at least begin to model the kind of discussion that we think a free and open democratic society should be able to sustain.

Advocates of speech codes are right about some things. For

example, they are right that hate speech itself has harmful effects. Hateful speech itself restricts speech. When someone says something that dismisses everything that you have said, some people will rise to the bait and say, "Okay, I want to fight." Other people will say, "It is simply not worth it." Some other people, depending on their age and their prior experiences, may internalize it and come to see themselves as inferior and even unworthy of speaking back. Thus, even advocates of codes restricting speech may have concerns for free speech partly on their side. Of course, having a code that restricts speech seriously jeopardizes the ideal of freedom of speech, but creating an institutional climate in which it is possible and even at some level acceptable for people to say hateful things can silence people who otherwise would be participants in that discussion. Once we start with the recognition that there is a danger to free speech on both sides, we can have a more productive discussion.

Question: In *Breaking the Cycles of Hatred,* you list forgiveness as an inadequate response to collective violence because no one can be ordered to forgive: forgiveness must be granted, and to expect forgiveness from victims is to revictimize them. However, for the societal scars of violence to truly heal, shouldn't forgiveness be an ultimate goal for all responses to violence, even if it is not required of initial collective responses as you suggest?

MM: I have struggled to try to articulate what the alternatives are to vengeance on one side and forgiveness on the other. It is a good question to ask, What's so bad about forgiveness? Isn't that the goal? When I started researching this question and I tapped into the great resources of Harvard libraries, I found that there was very little written about forgiveness. The only material I found when I started writing about forgiveness in 1996 was in the Divinity School library. There were very strong and powerful writings about forgiveness in various theological traditions, but people in the different religious traditions disagreed over whether forgiveness should be granted before there has been contrition by wrongdoers. Different traditions have very different views about that. Some think it is the granting of forgiveness that could be the triggering act for the change of the wrongdoer. Others feel strongly that forgiveness should not be given until there has been a change by the one who committed a wrong. It struck me, as a very basic point, that we could recapitulate some of the very conflicts that we are trying to avoid if we emphasize forgiveness, because there are different religious views about forgiveness.

Second, whatever forgiveness may mean in these different traditions, there seems to be commonality in the recognition that forgiveness involves the victims' relinquishing their sense of resentment, however rightfully it was earned. Let's look at that carefully. If it is relinquishment by victims, then it has to be voluntary. To be told to forgive, to be expected, to be forced, is no longer voluntarily to relinquish your resentment. I have talked with many people who have testified in the Truth and Reconciliation Commission hearings, the Human Rights Commission hearings in South Africa for the Committee on Human Rights. Many of the survivors observe: "I was open to the idea of forgiveness, but the wrongdoer came forward with his hand stretched out expecting me to forgive. I took that as a personal insult. Why? It is up to me to decide to forgive." This kind of response really made me think about how wrong it is to assume or expect forgiveness, especially from people who have been severely victimized. In a profound sense, the only thing that a victim of serious violence possesses immediately after the violence is control over his or her own response to that experience. If that response itself is taken away and the person is told, "Do not respond the way that you are responding. It is wrong for you to hold onto resentment," it seems to me a further deprivation, a further dishonoring of that victim.

Now there are extraordinary people who have been utterly victimized and nonetheless who do forgive. We should admire and honor those people. I do not know if any of you have had the chance to see the documentary about the Truth and Reconciliation Commission called *Long Night's Journey into Day*. If you have not seen it, I highly recommend it. Among other portions of this documentary that I find compelling is a close interview with a series of women, all of whom are mothers whose children were killed on a bus after an informant told the apartheid-era police that there were terrorists on the bus. There were no terrorists on the bus. There was a group of teenagers on the bus. So after apartheid falls and the Truth Commission process begins, these mothers go to the commission and hear the application for amnesty from the man who was the informant. As it turns out, this man was himself a black-skinned African. All the mothers are also black-skinned Africans. In the interviews before they meet together, the mothers—to a person—say, "I will never forgive him. I will never forgive him. How could he do this?" They meet with him and they yell at him. And they say, "How could you do this? How could you turn against your own people? How could you turn against these teenagers? They were innocent!" Some of the mothers are crying, but most of them are yelling. This man who has applied for amnesty has his head in his hands. He apologizes, but he is clearly in agony. One of the women who had adamantly declared "I will never forgive" suddenly says, "I forgive you." Then one by one by one all the other mothers forgive him. There is this extraordinary sense of recognition that they are all sharing a common humanity and will have to build South Africa together.

I should clearly state I am talking about forgiveness as an act of the individual victims. When we move to the societal perspective and talk about a society forgiving, there is a great danger of sliding quickly into amnesty, a legal form perhaps of forgiveness, or perhaps it is simply a mechanism to wipe away the option of prosecution. This has only a family resemblance to the forgiveness I have been describing. There is an enormous danger when you move to a societal form of analysis that that is what forgiveness ends up being. Amnesty is really not about relinquishing resentment; it is about politically deciding it is not worth it or it is not justifiable to proceed. If you can develop an alternative way to frame forgiveness at a societal level, I would be interested to hear about it. I certainly support institutions like a truth commission that can encourage survivors to have occasions to encounter perpetrators and encourage perpetrators to acknowledge their acts and seek to make amends, and, yes, to make it possible for survivors to consider forgiveness. But anything beyond that is both internally contradictory and a further insult to survivors.

Question: Do you think military intervention is ever justifiable to prevent crimes against humanity?

MM: When I was in sixth grade, I had a great teacher who began the year by giving us two questions: "Do you think war is ever justified?" and "Do you think the weapons of the world should be destroyed?" So I wrote, "I think war is never justified and all the weapons in the world should be destroyed." We then spent several months studying wars for independence around the world, and then he asked us the same questions. I wrote, "I think war is sometimes justified, and I think the weapons of the world should not be destroyed if they are needed for defensive purposes." I would like to think that I have progressed since sixth grade, but I don't think I have very much.

Recently I served on the International Independent Commission on Kosovo, a commission that was created by the government of Sweden after the military intervention in Bosnia. As I agreed to serve on that commission with representatives from eleven other countries, I said, "You should know I was against the military intervention." The chairman, Judge Richard Goldstone from South Africa, said, "That is fine. We have people with all kinds of views on this commission." In the course of the commission's work, I certainly heard a lot of testimony and learned about not only the actions of Slobodan Milosevic, but also what was known at the time of the intervention about something called Operation Horseshoe. That was an effort, planned by the Serbian government, to remove Kosovar Albanians from their homes.

In light of that and other evidence, I came to the conclusion that the military intervention was justified, but I and the other commissioners also had no doubt that the intervention was illegal. It was done in a way that violated the procedural steps necessary for international community approval. It was done in violation of international law. Plans to fly missions at a height at which it was not possible to control against civilian death are potential violations of international law. Proceeding without approval of the Security Council made the intervention an act of unauthorized hostility. The commissioners all concluded that there was a powerful justification for humanitarian intervention, and nonetheless the intervention as pursued was illegal. That presented a real challenge in our deliberations. How should the gap between justification and legality be addressed? Do we close that gap by changing the law? Or do we close that gap by changing our conceptions of legitimacy? On this score I think movement has to be obtained in both directions. Precommitments to legal procedures should not lightly be tossed aside. But in light of new experience, we can change the law for the future. We also need to acknowledge that the deck is stacked against humanitarian intervention as long as unanimous UN Security Council advance approval is required.

Question: Earlier you mentioned that there is a big difference between the practical and ideological aspects of war. As Americans, we often rely on thinking of war as an ideological issue because we are not as familiar with the practical aspects and instead see it romanticized in movies. Do you think that there is a way to bring to people a real consciousness and understanding of war on a very practical level? Would that change their minds about being so willing to invade other countries?

MM: There was a thought experiment somebody had not long ago that I thought was pretty good. If in order to launch a war a public official had to actually press a button that was implanted inside the body of a human being, and the only way to actually press the button was to cut open the human being, that could bring home the fact that human beings will die when that button is pressed. This is just a thought experiment, but it is a good one. At the moment there is no immediate experience of killing or of death for the president or the Congress who authorize war.

In contrast, it is striking that the military in America are the least enthusiastic about the war. People who have actually had experience with war are not in favor of starting a new one. To think about institutional, practical, and imaginative ways to bring home the reality of war to the people who make the decision seems to me an awfully good idea.

When *The Children of Heracles*, a Euripides play, was recently produced at the American Repertory Theatre in Cambridge, there was a brilliant and courageous decision made not only to produce a play that deals with the issue of refugees but to produce it in a contemporary setting. A further inspired decision was to involve real refugees in the production. Many students from a local high school who are themselves refugees became involved in the production and appeared each night. The producers tried to make this play function the way theater did at the time that Euripides wrote, when theater was about contemporaneous politics. Theater was about creating an arena where citizens could actually see and debate the issues of the day. Here, in the Cambridge production, the play was introduced each night by a panel discussion including a refugee and an observer of the current political or historical context. This helped make the play seem immediate and urgent and generated extensive audience discussion about living through war and loss. It is hard to think about going to war in the abstract after such discussions. The combination of personal stories, dramatic narratives, and structural analyses could motivate people to think and behave with more attention to human consequences.

Question: How can we develop international bodies that deal more with issues related to national sovereignty and possibly work towards developing international law or even an international conception of morality?

MM: The most important contributors to the development of the
ideas and even the practices of public international law for the
last fifty to seventy years have not been governments; they have
been nongovernmental actors. They have been grassroots organizations and international nongovernmental organizations.
These NGOs have been important both in articulating the content of these ideals and also in creating processes of monitoring,
exchanging, communicating, pressuring, and shaming behavior.
As it turns out, the intellectual force and the muscle in the movement for international human rights is not in governments and
not in the UN. There is something very exciting about that because it suggests that actually there is power in the weak. In fact,
the powers of the weak over time may be more powerful than the
powers of the strong. Those people who work for governments
and the UN have enormous sets of constraints about what they
can do, what they are willing to do, and what they are politically
able to do. People who do not have all those obligations may have
more freedom, more ability to maneuver.

Do I think we should withdraw support for the UN and other
formal public institutions? Absolutely not. Those are important
focal points and foils. International criminal prosecutions in the
ad hoc tribunals have their limitations, but they have jump-
started debate and institution building at the national level to
recognize and enforce human rights. These international criminal prosecutions reveal a sense of normative urgency and a
sense of institutional creativity, thereby reflecting and in turn
stimulating action by various people around the world. If those
formal institutions work, they will only work because of the role
of the nongovernmental organizations. The best prospect for
dealing with the tensions between national sovereignty and the
goal of international human rights is working through interna-

tional nongovernmental organizations that, by their very nature and identity, transcend the boundaries of any nation-state, as do multinational corporations. A promising response to globalization in its corporate form is growth in civil society, which takes a comparable international, transborder form.

Question: Should people who hope to make a positive difference in the world follow in your footsteps and get law degrees?

MM: My advice is not to go to law school. Law school makes sense, as was true in my case, if you think that the materials you want to spend time using your mind to grapple with are legal materials. If you have a passion for law or if you think that you really want to litigate or that this will give you the kind of credibility you will need in settings that you want to go, by all means go to law school. But if you are looking for a way to make a difference in the world around these issues, the more immediate and greater need is to affect the consciousness of people. Law is a limited means for doing that. It would be far more effective to write screenplays or to work on elementary school curricula.

Ask yourself, What have been the most influential experiences in shaping your ideas about the world, about violence, about human dignity? What are the images that you have? What are the ideas that you have? Events unfolding in history may be the most indelible in people's minds. But also influential are images from mass media, and here I am thinking of film and television as much as news. I have several students who have earned law school credit for writing screenplays, and even one who sold one. Write plays. Write fiction. Write journalism. Produce rock videos. Figure out ways to affect people's consciousness.

SWANEE HUNT, diplomat

Swanee Hunt is founder and chair of Hunt Alternatives Fund, a private foundation advancing innovative and inclusive approaches to social change at local, national, and global levels. In addition, she is the director of the Women and Public Policy Program at Harvard's Kennedy School of Government, where she also teaches. During her tenure as U.S. ambassador to Austria (1993–97), Hunt hosted negotiations and several international symposia to focus efforts on securing peace in the neighboring Balkan states. Her work in Europe prefaced the creation of Inclusive Security: Women Waging Peace, which advocates for the full participation of women in formal and informal peace processes. Ambassador Hunt, a member of the Council on Foreign Relations, writes a nationally syndicated column for Scripps Howard News Service and is author of This Was Not Our War: Bosnian Women Reclaiming the Peace. *Hunt talks about her experience in Austria, the roles women play in peacemaking activities, and the challenges they face when they step up to the plate.*

Question: Would you tell us how you became involved with questions of international security and peacekeeping?

Swanee Hunt: I left Dallas, where I was born and raised, because I didn't thrive there. After traveling and living in Europe for four years, I studied theology. I ended up spending sixteen years in Denver, Colorado. There I helped start a women's foundation to generate more funding for projects relating to economic self-sufficiency for women and girls. While starting my own foundation, codirecting a halfway house for mentally ill clients, and serving as a minister of pastoral care, I became a big believer in

providing others with the support they need to identify and im-
plement their own solutions rather than imposing solutions from
the outside.

Getting to know Bill and Hillary Clinton during the 1992
presidential campaign, I thought, "At last, we're going to have
people in the White House who understand the kinds of issues
I care about, particularly the inner city." Hillary in particular
wanted me to play a role in the government. I thought I would
work on welfare reform—one of the issues I'd helped with in
Colorado. Instead, I became U.S. ambassador to Austria. There
were very few women in high-level foreign policy positions, and
I had a decent grasp of German, so off I went.

In Vienna I looked around for the inner city and discovered it
was where people went for the flakiest croissants and the richest
coffee you ever had. I'm not sure how they do it, but the Austri-
ans don't have very serious social problems like the ones that I'd
worked on in Denver. But they had seventy thousand refugees
coming over the border.

This was 1993. Bosnia was a brand-new country; it declared
its independence just before it was attacked. The Serbs under
Slobodan Milosevic were making a play for Greater Serbia. They
were trying to push non-Serbs out, using atrocities to make them
flee. People from our embassy—we had five hundred employees
—were doing some of the refugee interviews. They were hearing the kind of terrible stories you read about in the Holocaust—
scenes such as a grandfather being forced to eat the liver of his
murdered grandson.

I sat at my big mahogany desk in Vienna saying, "Oh, but I'm
busy with a trade commission coming in to deal with the pros
and cons of genetically modified soybeans or a Viennese exhibit

of an American sculptor. Why should I be dealing with something happening in another country?" After a while I couldn't live with myself. I suggested to the State Department that our embassy in Austria host the U.S. Embassy for Bosnia, since it was too dangerous to open an embassy in Bosnia. So for a year and a half, the American embassy for Bosnia was actually in Vienna, inside the embassy I was running.

I ended up hosting negotiations between two sides in the three-way conflict, since the Bosnian Croats and the Bosnian Muslims were fighting each other as well as the Serbs. We felt if the Muslims and Croats could come together, they could face off the Serbs. In the course of those negotiations, which lasted about seventeen days, about sixty people were coming in and out—lawyers and politicians and the like. There was not one woman, even though the former Yugoslavia had the highest percentage of women PhDs of any country in Europe.

How could you end up with no women out of sixty people in these negotiations? I found this striking, given my experience in Colorado helping start the women's foundation and seeing the innovative things women were doing at the grassroots level. As I got deeper and deeper into trying to figure out where the women were, I realized that the women were doing all kinds of things to try to stop the conflict and hold their communities together, but they were not represented on the negotiating team.

A little while after I came to the Kennedy School of Government, I started looking at other conflicts and noticing the same dynamic. It was always guys in gray suits. Some of these were wonderful guys, but it was striking to me that there were never women on the negotiating teams. When I asked about it at the UN, an official said, "In Africa the warlords won't let women be on the team because they're afraid the women will compromise." I thought, "You know, that is the point of negotiation." It seemed to me that this was not simply a feminist cause. This was about securing stability as quickly as possible by bringing around the table the people most highly invested in that stability. Often they are the people who have not been planning the wars, who are less concerned about territory than they are about stopping the violence, who are accustomed to working outside of the system to find innovative ways of addressing these problems. Remember, by the time war breaks out, you have a failed situation. You need people who can think outside the box. Yet those people are, in fact, excluded from the negotiating table.

I realized this could actually be very important; this might be a lasting contribution I could make. At that point I was forty-five and starting to think, "Well, the next twenty years are the big twenty. What difference can I make in the world?" If I could change the way policy makers work on issues of war, that would be the greatest contribution I could make.

Question: Does there need to be a shift in identity in order for women to continue to gain power in political decision making? Do they need to learn to block and tackle? Do they need to be like bullfighters?

SH: In the seventies, we thought that if a woman is going to have a place in the corporate boardroom, she should look as corporate as she can. What does corporate look like? Well, *corporate* means no ruffles. You have to make yourself look like the men. It is not just what you're wearing, it's also your voice and whether or not you learn to interrupt. Men are really good at that. Should women learn to push? That's the block-and-tackle part. I've worked very hard learning to do that. I'm not proud of it. I wish that weren't the way it is.

When I work with graduate students, especially the women, I tell them to get their voices down and strong and stop saying "just": "I just want to ask this question," "I sort of think that maybe I'll just save the world . . . ," all those disempowering ways of speaking. The packaging matters a lot.

But the question is, At what point do you lose the value you added by becoming too much like the guys that you're trying to fit in with or make comfortable? Much of this is human nature. The reason guys ask other guys to be on a board of directors instead of asking women to be on the board is that they want to have someone they're comfortable with. These aren't bad guys. So to your question, the basic answer is yes, women do have to learn to block and tackle. I wish it weren't so.

The other piece is that women need to stay in touch with other women so that we don't lose appreciation for who we are as women. I held a meeting at the State Department to thank a number of women who had helped me as I moved into that new world. They were high-level: assistant secretary and higher. There were about eight or nine of us around the table. There was almost a yearning that I heard from them. They said, "We never see each other. This is like what we did when we were in our twenties. We are starved for this—being able to talk to each other about the challenges we face as women." Women can make a big mistake by cutting themselves off from that camaraderie.

Question: In "Inclusive Security: Women Waging Peace," you write that "Rather than motivated by gender fairness, this concept is driven by efficiency." How would you respond to the feminist argument for total equality among the sexes and rejection of gender stereotypes, since your argument is based on a certain degree of differentiation?

SH: I understand the concern about gender differentiation. I come from a family that is in the oil and gas industry where the boys of every generation are trained to go in and run the company and the girls are trained to marry a boy who will run the company. I have lived under and chafed under that discrimination. I have very strong views about gender fairness and how differentiating puts us in boxes that are confining.

But when I go out into the field, whether to Rwanda or Guatemala or Cambodia, and I sit down and talk with women like Nanda Pok, who has organized over five thousand women to run for office in Cambodia (and, by the way, one thousand of them have been elected)—I say, "Nanda, why do you think it's important to try to get women to run for office?" She says to me, "Because we women see things differently from the way men do." Now I can't tell you if that is nature or nurture or a combination. I don't think that is the important question here. I have asked that question probably four hundred times, and out of four hundred, I have probably found three women who didn't say to me, "We women see things differently in this conflict." I am reporting firsthand accounts instead of trying to be true to a feminist critique of gender differentiation.

Question: How are you working to make women more organically involved in governance and negotiation and not an afterthought or last-minute requirement?

SH: Academia provides an extraordinary opportunity; it leverages change. I have a number of choices about how to spend my time. Through my private foundation, I can fund my own projects. But to invest in students who go out and become the members of Congress, become the secretaries of Commerce or Education back in their home countries—that's an extraordinary opportunity.

I care every bit as much about reaching men as I do about reaching women. One of the frontiers of understanding is the effects of hormones on human behavior. For example, some are positing that testosterone may make a person more aggressive and more convinced that he will prevail. If you think more highly of yourself, you are liable to go into battle because you think you will win. If you take a group of men and women, and after they have had some time to get to know each other you ask everybody to give a number ranking the competence of everyone in the group, including themselves, the men will tend to rank themselves higher than the others rank them, and the women will rank themselves lower.

Apply that finding to the question of women's leadership, and you will see that we have a two-pronged task. We need to help women figure out how to overcome what may be not just socialized but also a biologically driven fear or self-deprecation. We then need to help men understand that there must be room for the women. The education has to happen on both sides, and they are equally difficult.

If I were to bring Aloisea Inyumba in from Rwanda and say, "Aloisea, talk to these people," she would come and say [very softly], "Oh, thank you, Ambassador Swanee for having me. It is such a privilege to be here, and I appreciate it so much that you are willing to listen to me." That is where she would start. Aloisea Inyumba was born in a refugee camp in Uganda, after her father was killed. When the 1994 genocide happened, Aloisea was twenty-six years old, and she had a college degree in social work. As you recall, 800,000 Tutsis and moderate Hutus were killed. Aloisea is Tutsi. She was appointed minister for gender and families in the aftermath of the genocide. She had to help figure out how to bury 800,000 corpses to avoid another health crisis on top of what had already happened. There was no heavy equipment, just machetes and maybe some hoes. Another big challenge was that in this country of 8 million people, there were 500,000 orphans. She started a nationwide campaign: "Everyone take one." That is all she said: "Everyone take one." You were to take whatever child was given; it didn't matter if that child was Hutu or Tutsi. She then became governor of the Kigali Ngali Province and was in charge of reintegrating 100,000 of the genocide perpetrators who had been released from the prisons. They were released back into the very communities where they had perpetrated the genocide. She had to keep these 100,000 from being massacred as they were released. She is a giant of a woman, a Martin Luther King character. Yet if she were to walk in, she would say meekly, "Oh, thank you." So how do we change that? Is it through the media? Through education? Through parenting? I don't know the answer, but it is a very serious question.

Question: You have argued that we must take into account not only weapon stockpiles but also concern among women that regime change may mean a change to Islamic fundamentalist leadership. How do these factors influence your perspective on the U.S.'s pending decision to invade Iraq?

SH: When I was in Vienna, I went to see a man who became my mentor. His name was Viktor Frankl. Frankl was a Holocaust survivor, and he talked about meaning as what drives you and keeps you alive. I said to him, "I don't know if I should stay in this job because I am so sickened by not being able to get the administration to intervene in Bosnia." I was advocating for military intervention. I was advocating for bombing. We were waffling. I wondered, "Should I resign from my position, or should I stay in it? Can I do more from the inside than I can from the outside?" Dr. Frankl said to me, "Madame Ambassador. Sometimes the right thing to do is only 55 percent right." It is one of the most important things anyone has said to me in my life. If you think about it, you do not know if you are on the side of the 55 or the 45 because if you have a position that is 45 percent right, you can make a fabulous case for that position. You can write essays, you can write books describing why that 45 percent is right. You do not know you are right until you look back, and even then you do not know. You are in a position where you have to commit or you are just paralyzed. He was trying to explain to me why people as good as those in the Clinton administration could be paralyzed by looking at the 45 percent and hearing all of the arguments against intervention. The Iraq situation is so complex that very good and thoughtful people disagree. If you are certain about your position on Iraq, you are probably not being very thoughtful, because this is one of the most devilish decisions that I have seen come around in a long time.

I hope that this wartime is creating a terrible sense of divine unrest in you. The greatest tragedy would be if watching the bloodshed and destruction and all of the unintended consequences, you say, "Well, I've had it with politics. I'm not getting involved in that scene. It's just dirty business." We have a paucity of imagination. That is our problem. We need new ways of thinking. That is why I try to bring others into the conversation. Let's get different people around the table. Of course you have to have the warriors around the table. You can't keep them away from the negotiating table. But why not double the number of chairs? Why not bring in some very different voices and see what happens when you change the mix?

Question: I understand the need to get women involved in negotiations that you describe, but if the goal is not so much gender equity in this case as it is promoting peace, it seems to me that at the same time we are promoting involving women, we should also be working to figure out why the people we choose to do our negotiations are not the sort of people that we should necessarily want to have involved in those negotiations.

SH: I have a very hard time figuring out how such smart people as those who conduct foreign policy could do something so stupid as to invite only the war makers around the table and say, "Now create peace." That seems so shortsighted. If you were mayor of Seattle, and you wanted to do something about smog, what would you do? You would bring together the car dealers and the environmentalists and the industry people, right? But you would also bring together the churches, the neighborhood organizers in the low-income community, the business leaders, and the education experts. In our domestic policy, we would never think of trying to bring together only two sides of the conflict and say, "Now we are going to come up with a solution." We would create a campaign to end smog in Seattle. For some reason that model, which is so basic in American policy making, has not transferred over into foreign policy making. It may be because the outsiders who are hosting the negotiations do not know many of the people who are on the inside really making the fabric of the society work. They only know the people who are fighting each other. It may be as simple as that.

Question: On the issue of getting involved in making a difference, for those of us who are not independently wealthy and may be facing just graduating from college, are there particular steps that you see as being important? We often question, Do I run for office? Do I teach? Do I become involved in nonprofit organizations? What do you see as being the most crucial steps to doing something about the way things are?

SH: I am always tempted to answer this question straight because you are asking it straight. I could make up something. I could say, "Well, it is really important to have different kinds of experience and understand how the society works from different perspectives. So I would recommend that you vary your life experiences and do this and do that, especially in your twenties. Blah, blah, blah . . ." But the truth is, you can make all the plans you want in terms of how you are going to get to there. And if you are a planner, please go ahead and make your plans. The chances of your life evolving according to your plan are probably less than 5 percent. Only do it if it is a comfort to you. Follow your passion and learn from the places that you get yourself into that you absolutely hate. You will probably learn more there. You will be miserable, but you will learn more about the way the world is dysfunctional while you are getting crushed in the middle of it.

My family bought a hotel in Fort Worth, and the manager was taking my sisters and me around to see how they had redone the hotel. We were taken up to the top floor and shown all the suites that were named for the leaders of Fort Worth history. There was Joe Smith and John Slaughter and so forth. After we looked into these seven suites, my sister Helen asked, "Where are the women of Fort Worth history?" The manager said, "Well, we looked for women, and there were not any who were doing anything important." So I hired a researcher, who in fact discovered that women had started the school system and the post office and the hospital while men were punching holes in the ground and slaughtering cows in the stockyards. I prepared a report about these great women of Fort Worth history. So the three sisters, who actually owned 75 percent of the hotel, came back and said, "Guess what? Here are these three great women. We don't want to take away the suites from the men of Fort Worth history, but let's take the fountain in the lobby and we'll put up a plaque for these women." Easy solution, right? So there was some consulting between the brother and the manager, and the answer was no. The most interesting part of this story is that the three sisters who owned 75 percent of the stock said, "Oh." That was it. It was awful! It was one of those moments I look back on and say, "How on earth could we have just said, 'Oh, rats!'"

But I have been energized by that moment for thirty years, because it was such a failure. You do learn more from those moments of failures. Don't be afraid to go back into them to say, "Why did that feel so bad? What did I learn? What am I going to do differently in my life not just for myself but for other people who are having similar experiences?" If you can't take the things that are crushing to you or that are propelling you forward and draw from those forces the lessons on how you are going to live your life, then you are missing out on a basic connection that makes our lives really worthwhile.

Question: Do you have a closing word before we round things off?

SH: I will leave you with a picture of a woman named Sophia. She lived in a little town in Croatia. She was an old woman. Every day she had one job, to go at noon to the church, to take the ropes that were tied up on the wall, untie them, pull on the ropes, and ring the bells in the tower. During the war, in village after village, when the Serb forces came in tanks, they would shoot up all the houses of the Catholics, the Croats, and then they would end up at the church. They would go to the church and shoot up the church. At the very end they would shoot the tower. Then they would roll out, and it would now be a Serb town. This old woman whose church had been shot up, every day you would find her in the churchyard at noon. There was wood splintered everywhere, but in the middle of the debris, the big bell that had been in the bell tower was lying on its side on the ground. Sophia, this eighty-year-old woman, was bent over with her old gnarled hands grasping the clapper and swinging her arms, ringing the bell. I carry Sophia inside of me, and I hope you will. No matter what the circumstances in which you are working, in which you are living, your job is to keep your hands on that clapper, ringing the bell.

JENNIFER LEANING, physician

Shortly before this interview, Jennifer Leaning returned from a Physicians for Human Rights mission to Afghanistan, where her investigations of potential human rights abuses included visits to a prison holding Taliban forces. Leaning is professor of international health at the Harvard School of Public Health and director of the Program on Humanitarian Crises and Human Rights at the school's François-Xavier Bagnoud Center for Health and Human Rights. A founding board member of Physicians for Human Rights, she is an authority on questions of humanitarian crises, medical ethics in emergency settings, and humanitarian law. Her work has taken her to conflict zones around the world, including Somalia, the Democratic Republic of Congo, Rwanda, and the Chad-Sudan border. In these pages, Leaning offers strategies on how to stay alive in volatile situations and describes her own processes of risk assessment. She also reviews various public health measures that could defuse some of the conditions that breed terrorism.

Question: Some analysts have suggested that there might be a link between public health conditions and terrorism. In light of this, do you believe that the U.S. should direct more funding to programs aimed at immediate health conditions around the world, possibly at the expense of more long-term research programs of uncertain benefit or long-term benefit?

Jennifer Leaning: The response partly depends on how you evaluate and understand the phenomenon of terrorism. Let's put that question aside for a moment and think about the range of options available to people who have a sense of agency, a sense of the future, a sense of hope—let's get more primitive—a sense that they can protect their children from harm—and more primitive—a sense that they have a pretty good idea of where their next meal is coming from. There are hundreds of millions of people who live in great insecurity where they have no sense of a future and no sense that they can protect their children from harm. There are probably a third of the world's people, or several billion people, who are not sure where their next meal is going to come from. So if you take those two levels of insecurity—that is, food insecurity, affecting a third of the world's population, and physical and psychological insecurity, affecting hundreds of millions of people who are caught up in war, conflict, or the immediate postconflict setting—you have got to think, What are their options? What are they susceptible to in terms of malignant leadership, bad ideologies that seem to make sense, or an option that is thrown their way? There are a huge number of people in the world who can be entangled in various types of scapegoating or analysis so that they are not necessarily going to be very sound or profound in their reactions to issues or threats.

From a preventive standpoint, which is always the public health position, if we want people in the world to be making stable, productive choices towards life, towards a society that is relatively peaceful rather than one that works through vengeance, anger, and violence, we need to be able to improve their condition, so that at the *first* moment they feel more secure, happier, with a greater sense of power and agency than they currently have. From that perspective, which looks at public health in the largest sense of promoting human security (and I think actually the inputs of public health are fundamental in promoting human security), investments in water, agriculture, sanitation, education, and transportation improve quality of life at the most basic level, making people feel that they are okay in their own lives and their own places.

Let us take a leap now to terrorism, and I am not an expert in this. I would say that the United States public is still pretty ignorant about terrorism, and in a way that is wonderful. In a way, it is a terrible loss of our innocence and our sense of comfort in the world that the Federal Emergency Management Agency is now talking to us about masking tape and plastic to put over our windows in case of a chemical or biological attack, that we now have to be worried about any large building or hotel or major hospital, particularly if they have the word "Jewish" in them or if they have a name that has Hebrew origin. All of these issues are really new in terms of the sense of urgency, and that is an appalling about-face in our world circumstance. I completely understand people in the elite and general public who are so angry about having this carpet of innocence and insurance ripped out from under them that they are going to label and brand and target and go after the people we call terrorists.

We could talk about the ethics of terrorism. I do not remotely endorse it, but I do believe it is pretty important to try to understand that millions of people elsewhere in the world have a very different view of this country, and a very different view of how it is that they can make a better life for themselves. It is important for us to understand that, and this is where I think the two links come together. If we are ever again to re-create the innocence and certainty in the future that we had just a few years ago, we are going to have to extend a sense of human security to other people elsewhere. This is the blowback about globalization. We are never going to be able to be isolated and okay. We are only going to be okay if others are more okay than they are now.

Question: What do you see as the relationship between doctors, lawyers, and economists in questions of international public health?

JL: We have a lot to learn from each other—doctors, lawyers, and economists. None of those disciplines really prepares a person to understand the problems of globalization. If we had here a doctor, lawyer, and economist, each classically trained, articulate, moderately well traveled—they had been to Florence but not to Kosovo—the first thing I would want them to acknowledge is that from within their discipline, they only know a very small part of the problem. To figure out what we need to do, people have to be synergistic and multidisciplinary. They have to be able to sift evidence from a variety of sources and value the information that comes in different packets.

For example, these experts have to be able to read the testimony from somebody who has been subjected to torture and understand the perspective that that person is struggling to bring to bear with the courage it takes to tell his or her story as well as an economic analysis of what debt burden is in much of West Africa. In addition, they must be able to understand what it means for a family in southern Africa to be faced with the three endemic and epidemic scourges that now all come together— HIV/AIDS, tuberculosis, and malaria—and what that combination of scourges presages for their life and future together as a nuclear family—over the next ten or fifteen years—in terms of behavioral constraints and the risk of death. A child who has already passed the threshold of having to worry about malaria now enters a threshold of having to worry about HIV/AIDS. In these

contexts, an eight-year-old girl is preyed upon by older men because the thought is that she does not have HIV/AIDS yet and is
safe, and there is a myth out there that if you have sex with a vir-
gin who is not HIV positive it will *cure* you of HIV/AIDS. There
are layers of jeopardy and disease and predation and morbidity
that a physician, having learned about what is happening in
southern Africa, will understand. But if this is just a physician
who has been born in and brought up in this country and is going through a classical training at the local hospital, unless he
or she has ears open to what is happening outside, this physician
is not going to be particularly helpful in addressing these problems of globalization and world change. The case is similar for
an economist or a lawyer. I won't go into the detail on that, but
you can see my line of reasoning.

Jumping ahead and saying international health entails situations where there is poverty, very little economic growth, and little understanding of democratic processes, let alone structures
that support a rule of law, who goes first, the doctor, the lawyer,
or the economist? I think it is the only reasonable answer to say
that people have to go there together and analyze what the issues
are and figure out the set of priorities. In analyzing it, not all situations of poverty and misery are the same. In Kosovo, after the
war and the expulsion into Albania/Macedonia, when the Koso-
vars then returned to their very small country, which had been
subjected to about two and a half months of bombing, the principal first problem was a security problem. There were gangs
roaming around, a lot of machine guns in the wrong hands, no
police forces, and land mines all over. The main issue was dealing with security. The second big issue was rebuilding the roads.
Nobody could communicate, nobody could travel anywhere,

and there were no telephones. It was extraordinarily difficult even to set up a meeting to organize something because it took you an hour to cross town (people basically abandoned vehicles and would walk because the roads were so bad). So a lawyer, a physician, and an economist looking at the immediate postwar reconstruction in Kosovo would have said the first problem is security, the second problem is transport, and the third problem— this is where the health focus comes in—is clean water.

If you were looking at the situation in Afghanistan, another postwar situation, you would see that the first problem here, in addition to security, was transport, because there was no access to health care due to bad or nonexistent roads. They had a rural population trapped in the mountains with appalling health indices. The only way you could get them to even the remotest expertise was if you had a transport system. I am talking about roads that would accommodate donkeys.

However, in Kosovo, two additional years post-reconstruction, the principal issue is, How do you kindle and ignite economic growth in a tiny place that does not clearly have a market niche? And how do you construct a legal system that is going to create a sense of ethics, stability, accountability, and fairness in a country that has been oppressed and contaminated by all kinds of crummy processes? In Kosovo at this time, I would say a public health person is less important than those who understand how to create legal systems appropriate to that society and background and economists who know how to jump-start fairly peculiar and distorted economies. This is a long way of saying that these three kinds of professionals are probably the three important ones you would need. I would actually like to have an engineer with me in trying to improve the situation in many parts of the world, but with an engineer, a physician, a lawyer, and an economist, assuming they were broad-gauged and open to different kinds of evidence and input, I would say you could do a lot.

Question: Often a good solution to solving health-related problems and epidemics in times of crisis is to educate the people themselves; for example, teach them how to protect themselves from disease or filter water for drinking. What is being done to teach people how to help themselves in these situations?

JL: A key component in public health—which actually could be borrowed and expanded into virtually any social enterprise—is to educate the general public. Public health is about the health of populations, the health of large groups; it is not about the health of individuals. When you are thinking about the approach to populations, the fact is that you cannot order everybody around all the time, so you will want to get some cooperation and some compliance. In addition, given the chance, human beings are going to want to protect themselves and care for the people they love, and given a slightly better chance, if they are not angry and filled with vengeance, they are going to have a more general social sense of probity and kindness. If you approach populations that way and you want to get them to do something, the fundamental strategy is education.

In public health and disasters, it is turning out to be absolutely critical for those in charge of the response and rebuilding to tell people what is going on honestly; say when you do not know something, and do your best to find out the answer (if it is a reasonable question); tell people what it is that they can do to take charge of their own lives and protect their families and friends and their community groupings; say when you are going to come back with a new message and a new engagement so people can park their questions as they accumulate and have faith that you are going to come back and talk with them again; have the people who are doing this communication be a combination of leaders the people have previously trusted (do not try to do this with a new leader); and have this public form of education linked to an expert, because not all the problems that come up in public health mode in a crisis setting are problems that a regular leader is going to be expert in.

Actually a really good model of this—that is, emergency public health education in a crisis setting—is Rudy Giuliani after the World Trade Center disaster. He was largely responsible for public health education: "Do not go down here, we are worried about the air, this building is unsafe, this area is off-limits, this is what we are doing to try to find people, this is what we are going to do about identifying remains, this is what we are going to do to help those of you who have been in a whole range of ways disadvantaged or made to suffer as a result of this event." Everything Giuliani did underscored the fundamental principles that we have learned over time about leadership in crisis. If you recall, he was there in front, but most often flanked with the fire chief, the police chief, engineers, heads of public health, city pathologists, the chief mortician, and the head of the morgue. First, he would give a speech in which he would update people with the latest information. He would be asked questions, and he would say, "Let me turn to so-and-so," and he would bring that person to the microphone and give that person the strength and visibility of being the expert, and you would hear it directly from the expert. When another question would come in, he would resume and come back. He did not leave the expert hanging for questions that were not related to that expert's area of expertise. He would give credit—another significant aspect of education in crises—to the people who were helping him and helping the general public; he did not try to hold himself up as the one essential leader. That particular mode of public health education in crisis would be critical in any setting that you could accomplish it.

One of the big problems in postconflict or crisis settings is that there is no television; there is not the technology to communicate immediately with large numbers of people. The moment you can, you should. For example, Afghanistan has a radio system with communication links going to the remotest mountains, and speaking through the radio is a critical way of bringing together a community of twenty to twenty-five million people. Similarly, in settings where there is no capacity for any kind of electronic communication, it is important to have a combination of runners, people who actually run out and tell the word, and flyers or print media.

When you are dealing with an extended crisis, it is crucial to give the household heads and the women a sense of empowerment about what they can do in the short run and the longer run to protect their families and find the support—including food and water and shelter—that they need. But in that education process, you have to keep in touch with them and say, "We are going to come back and listen to your questions." You have to have a process for a two-way street, even at the most primitive level of communication around town meetings.

Public health education in a crisis setting is extremely important. We have learned a lot of lessons about how to do it well. It needs to be technology dependent, and it needs to be culturally

and socially appropriate, in terms of being responsive to the issues and preoccupations that people have.

Question: I was hoping that you could describe for us the process by
which you were able to get the information to report on the conditions of the Taliban prisoners.

JL: The way you do these kinds of missions is to first of all get a vi-
sual geography in your mind about what the terrain is like. You
go to movies. I went to see *Seven Days in Tehran* just to see what
Tehran looks like. You talk to people who have been around and
come back. You have a very developed sense of pattern recognition that comes with experience. I knew that an air war with special forces all over the country, moving fast, with an at least
disputably criminal set of allies, that is the Northern Alliance,
was going to wreak havoc on the civilian population, and that
there were going to be violations of human rights and international law. I knew it. You get in the country, and you talk to the
International Committee of the Red Cross (ICRC), which is a
very important international institution that in most places in
the world has been there for the duration of the conflict and has
very good information about certain issues. The reason they
have good information is that they do not talk to people like me;
they talk only to the government and only to the warring parties.
They are very valuable, but they are not whistle-blowers. So I
went to the ICRC and I said, "I have concerns about the campaign in the north of Afghanistan: a lot of airpower, tons of
people surrendering, all kinds of civilian villages apparently
bombed, rapid movement of the Northern Alliance through
these areas down to Kabul. There are probably some issues up
there, right?" In this case, the ICRC said it might be worth going up there to look. That was the green light.

As you move into these areas, you have to be careful, quiet, and nonflamboyant. But you follow every possible lead and you do not sleep much, and you make sure that you take care of a few things: water, some food, and periodically some rest so that you are thinking. You are taking notes all the time in some way that is not easily discernible. My handwriting is bad enough that I do not have to go into code, but there are ways in which you have to be careful about the discoverability of what you are finding and how you are talking to people. It helps to be a physician who is trained to ask detailed questions with a sense of logic and fact but who is also interested in how people are feeling, so they do not feel they are talking to a lawyer. As a physician, you are also very comfortable with the issue of confidentiality which you pledge to people. By your deportment and the way you stay away from issues that are not in your line of sight, they realize you are not in there for some sob story or to find out how much money they have. They realize that you actually have a question about what happened to them, and then they relax about all the other extraneous things they may be worried about. They will answer questions about what happened.

The other thing about being a trained professional—I am not saying you have to be a physician—is that you have a certain competence about how you are going to interact with other kinds of trained professionals. I have a lot of respect for military commanders and custodial types in the armed services: fire, police, and prison commandants. They have very hard jobs. I approach them respectfully and figure out a way to get to talk to the people I am interested in that is not going to threaten their overarching sense of their command and their ongoing endurance in that position. The way I got access to the prison was to say that I was a physician, that we had heard there were terrible health conditions in the prisons, and that we were hoping to find out about these conditions and generate public support so that there might be a way of creating more resources and making it easier to take care of the prisoners. I did a little bit of advance checking to make sure that was not going to blow up in my face as an entry point, but it turned out to be okay. Then you just have to have a certain amount of assurance that they are not going to stop you. There are only certain kinds of people that you would dare to do this with. You do it with people who have a standing in a community, a reputation to uphold; they have some leadership and a group that follows them, and then around them there are people who say, "Yeah, he is in command, and we will give him that." You do not have this kind of interaction going down a dirt road with somebody you know is a drug runner, a rapist, a criminal, someone who does not keep his word at a certain level of professional interaction. When I am dealing with people I know I can't trust at that level, I am *very* careful about when I see them, with whom, and under what circumstances.

Question: What is your thinking process before you even decide to leave in terms of how much danger you are prepared to face?

JL: It is partly a cost-benefit assessment. How high do I think the risk is? I think it through quite carefully and then ask: "What would be the benefit of getting this information or bearing witness and coming back and being able to provide another window onto what is happening?" In a setting of human rights and international law, it is always the case that the full story never comes out. Sometimes it takes fifty years for 80 percent of the story to come out. Think about the stories you read in the *New York Times* or the stories that are still unfolding about World War II.

You may only read these stories in the obituaries, as there are a lot of people who were prominent from World War II who are now dying. The *New York Times* does a lot of historical work for the obituaries; they are biographies, and you are not going to find some stories anywhere except in the obituaries.

What I am interested in is getting more of the full story about the human rights issues: the violations of law, the behavior of groups and people in crisis settings. I am interested in getting that story out earlier, so that it is happening in time for those of us who are making the choices to know the information and have a more grounded and whole way of thinking through the next step and the next strategy. Understanding how our troops behaved in Afghanistan and the horrors that were inflicted on the prisoners of war is a very important corrective for the United States in terms of the phases of work they are going to be embarking upon, for instance, in Iraq. It is also important for Americans to know that you cannot just assume that the people you have elected are going to behave in all the fine details as well as you would like.

Human rights people are engaged in saying, "Yes, but...," particularly in a country where, within the United States, we have very good values, norms, laws, and often a good track record. But we are also the superpower, and it is really important for people in this time frame and for the next fifteen or twenty years (beyond that we are probably not going to be a superpower, but nobody seems to be planning for that) to be saying, "Yes, but..." Yes, Afghanistan was an important venture. It was good that the Taliban were kicked out; they were a repressive, awful, ridiculous regime, particularly in the last two or three years of their reign. They wound up being this debilitated theocracy that spent all of their time seeing how long a woman's garment was and whether she showed any ankle. If there was a cab going by with a tape deck, the driver was hauled off. But they were not doing any of the jobs of governance. On the other hand, the way in which we routed the Taliban and the way in which we are interacting with our allies there and with the prisoners leaves much to be desired for a conquering nation that wants to abide by the rule of law.

I try not to take risks that are very profound: I do not scuba dive; I am mistrustful of machinery I do not understand; I promised my family I would never go in a helicopter, because they are unforgiving machines and if something goes wrong, you are dead; if I am in an elevator and it jerks, I am out of that elevator and I will take the stairs. I am not a risk taker like that, but I am going to take reasoned risks that involve some planning, things I can understand and control. I feel I can understand a lot about people, and I trust my judgment on that, so where other people will take their risks with machines, I will take my risks with people.

Question: On the theme of risk taking, what risks are unique to human rights workers? Also, was there ever a time where you have had to draw a line in terms of your own safety even though it might have helped other people?

JL: In the last twenty years, the people on the outside, expats, are getting more and more numerous. What is becoming increasingly clear, whether you are a humanitarian person, a UN worker, a Red Cross worker, or a human rights person, is that if you are First World, whether you are white or a person of color, going into the Third World (I think the modern euphemism "developing world" is a phony phrase) to an area torn by big human rights abuses if not war, you are not safe. You cannot trust the fact that people are going to say, "Oh, great! You have come in to help us solve our problems!" That went out about twenty-five years ago.

So you have to be fairly careful about going in with a mission and figuring out why you are there. In human rights, you are there to understand a problem, investigate it, make a report, and then survive to talk about it when you come out. Your work is partly in-country, to create the sense of connection with the people who are suffering, so that they know that what is going on is not being utterly ignored, that there are reasonable people outside the Third World with whom they can connect and attach some hope. That is really important. But what you are actually, fundamentally trying to leverage is that when you come out, you can talk to the First World with a certain level of energy and authenticity and fact that is going to make the policy change. You have made a bad mistake if you have risked your life right up to the edge so that you get badly hurt or killed and you cannot come out to tell the story. So the injunction I give in human rights training is: survive in order to report. There is no need for any more martyrs; they don't cause a ripple. Martyrdom does not exist anymore.

My sense is that if you cannot be pretty sure that you can have a handshake with the people who are taking you up-country and with the people you meet along the way, if you cannot be pretty sure that they are going to respect who you are and give you a little space to do your work, if you cannot have that assurance, then you cannot do human rights work. Physicians for Human Rights is not in Iraq. In fact, there are very few human rights organizations doing anything in Iraq. It is too unsafe in general to move around; people are too wary, and they do not want to talk to you. In Iraq we would want to excavate the mass graves and have the families of the missing identify who was in those graves. To do that, you need to be in place and have an office in the city, with people coming in. You are incredibly visible. It is too hot a thing to do right now, given what is going on. So in human rights, there needs to be some stability of connection with the people that you need to rely on to get the information.

Question: As a physician, what perspective or particular concerns do you bring to the conversation about how best to utilize and distribute our resources?

JL: It begins with consciousness and awareness, which is one reason why this course at Harvard is very important. Over the last fifty years, since the end of the Second World War, the United States and the West have accentuated the gap between the rich and the poor and the gap in future potential and the gap in any sustainable sense of hope. In other words, we have developed in a large number of ways, and much of the world has moved very little, so the relative disproportion has gotten worse. The world has grown more crowded and also more complicated than it was post–World War II, but the fundamental point remains that there are an unacceptable number of people dying young and an unacceptable number of people dying in childbirth. Similarly, we can see the gap in the indices around health and water and food and education and hope—the expectation that one can have a reasonable life and can be secure in that life and have children and feel okay about oneself. That is not a set of expectations that large parts of the world can remotely hope to aspire to. Just realizing that differential is first of all the most important aspect of starting the next phase, which is, What are you going to do about it?

I would submit that whether you want to be a rock musician, a physician, or a nuclear physicist, part of what someone coming out of college must be challenged to say to himself or herself is, How is this going to make the world better for all these people who have very little? I am not speaking about another Albert Schweitzer initiative; the world is more complicated. Figuring out where you are fitting in and keeping an edge of discomfort *all the time* in your mind and in your heart and in your reading and in all your interactions is, to me, an essential part of being in this world now. We have no excuse not to recognize that we are unutterably privileged, and whatever flick of fate meant that you were born here and not in many parts of the world that I am speaking about does not give you any reason to think that they matter less than you do. Do things that make what I just said seem real to you: travel, dream, read, go to movies that are increasingly good about bringing these people home to you. And do not forget that all the sacrifice that your family has put behind you and all the work that you have done to be here—I respect it deeply, as I know how hard it is to be here and succeed here—is not going to amount to anything at the end of your time when your life is shut out if you cannot also say, "I did this for others as well."

There is a line in Yeats's autobiography that struck me as just unbelievable. This is sort of a mixed message, because I believe that Yeats, through his writing, has affected generations of us on this planet. He said, "When I think of all the books I have read, and of the wise words I have heard spoken, and of the anxiety I have given to parents and grandparents, and of the hopes that I have had, all life weighed in the scales of my own life seems to me a preparation for something that never happens." Part of that statement reflects that he was somewhat depressed. Part of it is that he was being somewhat manipulative—he knew damned well that he had done a lot. But part of it was, to me, that this was a man who had an ambition always to be changing the world as well as doing his craft, and he was not sure he had gotten the balance right. I might have said to him, "Yeats, I think you got the balance right." But that tension between who you are and who you are for others, I think, is an essential part of being alive today.

5. *RELIGION AND ETHICS*
In Search of Global Values

HARVEY COX, theologian

Harvey Cox is one of the most influential theologians of the twen-
tieth century. In 2005 Cox celebrated the fortieth anniversary of
his book The Secular City, *which has sold more than one million*
copies in more than fourteen languages. In this classic work, Cox
argued that God is as much at work in secular life as in formal
religion, especially when it comes to social justice. Cox has been
teaching at Harvard Divinity School since 1965 and is the author
of ten books, including, most recently, When Jesus Came to Harvard: Making Moral Choices Today. *He has written extensively*
on urbanization, world Christianity, Jewish-Christian relations,
and contemporary spiritual movements. In this interview, Cox
discusses the market economy in terms of its religious function,
the ethics of market values, and how much is enough.

Question: How did you become interested in questions of religion
   and ethics?

Harvey Cox: I grew up in a small town in southeastern Pennsylvania
   back in the 1930s. It was a very small town in which there was
   not a lot going on. But there were a lot of churches. There were
   fifteen hundred people, as I remember, and there were eleven
   churches. I got interested early on in different churches in our
   town, maybe because when I wanted to find something different
   to do in the evening, I would go to one of the activities—a dinner, a party, a choir concert, a lecture, a revival, something happening in one of the churches other than the one my parents
   belonged to. I quickly became interested in the question, Why
   do we have so many different churches? What are the differ-
   ences among them? What do they teach? How do you decide

which is the right one and which is the wrong one? Maybe they are all wrong; maybe they are all right in their own way. I don't remember a time when I was not interested in these subjects. Religion seems to me to be one of the most interesting subjects you could conceive of.

Now this was many years before Diana Eck's exposure of the much richer heterogeneous religious culture that we now have in America, not only the different Christian denominations in the little town I grew up in but also all the various world religions represented down the street and around the block. But my start was there, and my interest has expanded outward.

I still think that the study of religion is where the big questions come up: human destiny, the meaning of human life, what it is all about, good and evil, how to overcome them, what is worth doing in life and what is not. Some of the answers given to those questions have been questionable from my point of view, others not, but this is the area—religious studies—in which you are allowed to ask and explore the big questions.

Question: In "The Market as God," you discuss the God-like market as omnipotent and omnipresent and a force that no religion or sum of religions is likely to overcome. Is there anything that we as individuals or as a society should be doing to check the force of the market in our lives?

HC: Maybe I was a little pessimistic at the end of that article where I said that I did not see any religious movement or other kind of movement that could challenge the enormous power that the market—the market as God—seems to have acquired in our time and our society. Maybe there are movements that will challenge it.

I recently read a book called *Branded: The Buying and Sell-*

ing of Teenagers. It is about the way in which marketers and advertisers are increasingly targeting very young people—that is, children five or six years old—to make sure they get tied into one of the brand names early on so that they will be lifelong, you might say, addicts of that particular brand. One of the things they do is hire college graduates who have studied psychology to advise their businesses about what the anxieties, vulnerabilities, fears, and hopes of young children and adolescents are so that they can tie their product into that age group. If you are feeling lonely, just buy this product and you won't feel quite as lonely. If you are feeling too fat, you can take this, and you will get skinny. If you are feeling skinny, you can take this, and you will put on some weight.

The next step is to try to convince people who are now studying psychology not to go into this business of trapping young people into brand names, of using their talents for this nefarious purpose—being an acolyte to the God of the market—and hooking kids early on. Studies show the damage that these marketing campaigns do. Children lack a positive image of themselves, they get hooked into watching too many hours of television, they don't exercise, and far too many become obese.

Now there are also campaigns and programs to encourage young people, including teenagers, to just say no. In other words, do not make your choices on the basis of the kind of slick, commercial appeal of these products. Do not let them play to your fears, because it is really a false hope that this product is going to make you any less lonely. Just say no to it! If there is enough of a consumer movement against this kind of misuse of psychological research at our expense, the situation may change.

So let me tweak the end of that article, if I could, and say that maybe I was in a more-pessimistic-than-usual mood that day. I think there is still hope.

Question: Karl Polanyi, whom you quote, says there will be a double movement whereby society will prevent the disembedding of the economy. Is Polanyi's thesis correct, or can the market triumph over social relations, making us all commodities?

HC: Briefly, Polanyi's argument is that there have always been and always will be markets in every society, whether it is a little street vendor or a fair or a bazaar. However, in previous history, markets have been guided and checked by a range of other institutions—families, states, religious institutions, and customs. The markets have not been allowed to have the dominant role in forming the meanings or values of the society. What has happened in the past 150 years, he argues, is that the market has become the dominant institution of Western society and now increasingly all around the world. The market controls not just economic life. Let me underline that. The market affects not just economic life; it affects what we believe is important in life, what we are striving for, what we believe is wrong with us and the society, and what we are to do. In other words, the market is generating the values and meanings by which hundreds of millions of people are living.

I am arguing that this is the function, which, in many societies in the past, has been that of religion or that of God. The market is now God in that sense of the word. I think you are asking whether the battle is over. Is this a God who is never going to have any real contenders? I don't think so. I sense a growing restlessness on the part of many people with what the market values. The market values production, efficiency, competition, but the market does not have any value that it assigns to gentleness, to compassion, or to some of the things that we know from our own experience are not only important but vital to human life. I sense, especially among young people, a suspicion of the market —so much suspicion, for example, about television commercials that there is now a second wave of commercials trying to sell you things by using irony and self-caricature to build this suspicion into the commercial and disarm your criticism of it.

Still, I do not think, in the long run, human nature being what it is, that this kind of cheapening and evisceration of human values can last forever. I certainly hope not. We are in a stage now in which the market is utterly dominant. There is hardly anything challenging it, and it is even assigned a kind of messianic role: if only the market could be spread throughout all the world, then hunger would be gone; there would be democracy everywhere; there would be all these good things; and the market is the key to it all. But notice that in Christianity, Judaism, and some other religions, the Messiah has not come yet—or at least has not come back yet in Christianity and has not come yet in Judaism—and you are advised to wait patiently for the benevolent outcome. Well, a lot of people have been waiting for quite a while in many parts of the world, and the situation is getting worse and not any better, so their confidence in this particular messianic figure of the worldwide market is being undermined. We are beginning to see and will see a larger backlash against it. I certainly hope so.

Question: Could you elaborate on how you think the contest between the market and religion will play itself out? Also, what are the possible outcomes even after the conceivable backlash against the market system?

HC: I would not characterize it exactly as a contest between the market and religion, so let me reconfigure that a little bit. I am not suggesting that the market is God only as a metaphor. I am arguing that it *functions* in many parts of the world as a faith. Phenomenologically, it does what religions have most frequently done. It provides the stories, metaphors, symbols, rituals, myths, values, and meanings that religions have provided. It is functioning as a religion; so this is really a contest *among* religions. This is a battle of the gods.

Furthermore, I do not think that I should let religions get off so easy. Religions have also surrendered to some extent to the Market God. Just turn your television on late at night sometime and see the marketing of religion that goes on: selling God's favors, selling the favors of a particular spiritual tradition. I am afraid that churches, synagogues, and other religious movements can very easily be co-opted into a market vision of the world. So-called megachurches are springing up all over the United States—huge churches of five or six thousand people, many of them based on market surveys. You go into the community and talk to people, largely those who are not going to church, and you ask them what they like and do not like about church. You organize focus groups. Then you devise a sort of religious product that is going to meet the widest market niche, and you roll it out, and that is the megachurch.

We could also think about universities, which have begun to conceive of students as customers. There was a time in the university tradition, not so long ago, in which we were all colleagues, here as a learning community, learning together, listening to each other, and helping each other. More and more, the image that the university administrations are creating is this: we have a product that is education. We have a catalog, a sales force, recruiters, great colored brochures, and we also have customers who come and pay for the product. But what this does is to diminish, even evacuate, the human content of the relationship of teacher to student, of student to student, of an intellectual community. It makes it something cheaper. I strongly dislike that invasion into the university of the marketing mentality. When I started teaching, our work as faculty members was not so much directed by people from the development office. Now, we are asked by them to meet with this possible benefactor or that possible donor, and I try to be a good citizen and do what I can. Nonetheless, I feel that I have been enlisted, not only as a professor and teacher but as part of the sales force, in this case to get benefactors for the university.

Back to your question. I do not want you to think that I am suggesting a battle between bad market and nice religion. I think we need a market; the market is an essential institution in any culture or society. What I am criticizing here is the escalation of the market to the predominant meaning- and value-creating institution of the whole society, the market as God. And I do not want religion to get off as easy as the phrases of your question implied.

Question: You wrote that you did not think that this new religion of the market would inspire the international traditional religions to lead a new jihad or crusade. How have your opinions changed in light of September 11th and the response to it?

HC: At the moment I wrote that I was hoping, frankly, for a tiny little crusade, for a modest jihad, against the market religion by the traditional religions. I will come clean on that. I was hoping for a somewhat more confrontational attitude toward market values and the Market God on the part of existing religious institutions, where I find confrontation or critique sadly lacking. By and large, religious institutions are just going along with this juggernaut and not raising questions about how it debases human life and human values.

Now, once in a while, a little minicrusade breaks out. For example, not too many years ago, a market developed all around the world in human organs. If you happened to be a rich person from the Western world and you needed an organ, say a kidney transplant, it could be arranged. You could fly to India or Turkey or some other places and purchase a kidney for a modest price of several thousand dollars. The kidney would be taken from a poor person, usually a woman, who would be given a modest sum of money and told that she would be fine with just one kidney. And the market began to grow. At that point, some people began to say, "Wait a minute, is there anything in the world, anything at all, that should be excluded from the category of commodity?" I remember a couple of years ago teaching a course with Professor Alan Dershowitz and the late Steven Jay Gould in which we talked about this very subject, the sale and purchase of human organs. To my considerable surprise, when we asked the students how many of them thought it was perfectly okay, almost half of them said yes. They argued that if people are poor and they want to make some money and they want to sell their kidney, let them sell it; they have a perfect right to do so. For me, this position completely overlooked the enormous asymmetry in power between the people buying the kidneys and those selling them.

This was one instance in which the various religious communities of the world—Muslim, Christian, Jewish—said, "Here we have to say *no.*" The human body, created in the image of

God, is not to be put on sale; that is not something we buy and sell. There are some limits. Now, I think we ought to start drawing some other limits pretty soon. Who owns the sky? There was a movement a few years ago to put advertisements on satellites in the sky so that we would see them blinking, I suppose, for many, many years. That may mean transforming the sky into a commodity. No one, then, could look up into the sky on a starry night without seeing an advertisement for such and such a product. Think about it. I would like to see us begin to compile a list of things that we would like to see excluded, if not by law then at least by moral consensus, from the things that are for sale in the world. Start with that. Religious communities of the world can help with that question. What is valuable? What has value in life beyond what you have in a purchase-and-sale agreement?

Question: In addition to stating that people are treating the market as God, you also mention that the market, like other religions, is not subject to empirical proof. How would you respond to the criticism that people do not view the market as religion but as a scientifically proved theory? Could it be that, like evolution is a scientifically proved theory, people are just changing their minds about how the world really does work?

HC: That is a perfectly legitimate question. There are, however, many people in the world who have deep reservations about whether the market theory of how one organizes economies is, in fact, proven as the best theory for everybody. The people who have those doubts tend to be those who have not benefited from the global spread of the market economy but, in fact, have experienced in the last twenty or thirty years a widening gap between the concentration of wealth on the part of those who have and less and less on the part of those who don't have.

It is interesting to me how those who profit from the market economy tend to believe it is something that is self-evident; those who do not profit from it are the ones who have questions about it. There is an interesting epistemological question. How does that happen? How do you have that discussion? Consider Brazil. Brazil is the fifth- or sixth-largest economy in the world, the largest country in Latin America, and a country that has been described by the International Monetary Fund and the World Bank as their laboratory for how successful a market system would be. But now nearly everyone agrees that in Brazil this strategy has been a miserable and complete failure. Brazil has the widest disparity between rich and poor of any country in Latin America, and the third-largest of anywhere in the world. So now Brazil is trying a different strategy. For some people, that suggests that the proof is not quite in yet that the market economy is the solution to the whole business. At least, millions and millions of Brazilians feel that that is still an open question; they want to try something else rather than the market road to prosperity, success, and fulfillment.

Let me underline that I do not want to be understood as saying that there should not be markets in the world. I am talking about the overemphasis, the overexpectation, the overselling of the idea of the market economy as the elixir that will cure everything, as the God we can count on. The other reason I struck on the idea of God is that I remember being told when I was a kid that you may not see what God is doing now—it may look bad or wrong—but if you wait long enough, farther along, you will understand. You trust the providential hand, as it were, even though the evidence may go the other way; it requires an act of faith. It says in Hebrews 11, "Faith is the substance of things hoped for, and the evidence of things not seen [yet]." We are often asked to have that kind of confidence in the market. I think especially of the people who sell stocks.

"Well, the stock market is down this week, but it will go up again. Believe me, it will go up again."

"Why should I believe you that it is going to go up again? Maybe it is going to keep on going down."

"Well, in the past, it has gone up and down."

"Inevitability is not a very good argument."

Here is what I am saying: the question you raised about the contending ways of dealing with hunger, famine, unemployment, illness, and homelessness among enormous numbers of people around the world is certainly not solved yet. Regarding salvation through the religion of the Market God, I am a skeptic. If you are going to ask me if I am a believer, this is one God I just do not believe in. I am pretty close to being an atheist about the God of the market, but let's say for the moment that I am a pretty strong agnostic. I think the burden of proof has to be on the other side that it is really *the* solution.

Question: To what extent do we see the beginnings of a global civil religion, some set of symbols and rituals that would unite people across the globe, regardless of religious difference or nation-state difference? One might think of Gandhi, Nelson Mandela, or the Dalai Lama as the secular saints of such a possibly emerging global civil religion. Could such a global civil religion be a counterweight to the religion of the market?

HC: I think at least Gandhi and the Dalai Lama would be a little surprised to hear you characterize them as *secular* saints. Certainly not. What is important to me about these two enormously significant figures in our history is that they are, indeed, rooted in a particular religious tradition. Gandhi lived and died a Hindu but always said that it was Jesus's Sermon on the Mount that was the most important source of his life and his philosophy. As a Buddhist, of course, the Dalai Lama incarnates or embodies another whole view about what the good life is about. Being a Christian, I think we are at a moment in religious history in which we have an enormous amount to learn from traditions other than our own—in this case, the Hindu tradition and the Buddhist tradition—and we have the opportunity.

I think especially of Buddhism, which is the tradition of the Dalai Lama. Some years ago, I spent some time in Japan studying Asian religious movements and, especially, Buddhism. I went to Kyoto, which is the great temple city south of Tokyo, and I noticed there, in front of one of the temples, a statue of the founder of one of the Buddhist movements. It struck me that he looked rather like Saint Francis. He was wearing a ragged robe with a rope around his waist. He wore sandals, and he carried a walking stick. So I asked my companion, who spoke Japanese, to read the inscription on the base of the statue, which said, "If there is one thing that I have learned in life, it is how much is enough." I thought, "That was worth the whole trip to Japan." If you can learn during your lifetime how much is enough, you have really learned something very important, something that the Market God is never going to teach you. The gospel of the Market God is that you never have enough. You need more. The whole logic of the religion of the market is based on accumulation, growth, and expansion. But there is a wisdom in some of the other traditions—that of Saint Francis or Buddhist teachers or Hindu saints—that we desperately need as a kind of counteraction to the ethic of the Market God.

PETER SINGER, ethicist

Peter Singer's work in bioethics is debated around the world, and The New Yorker *has called him "the most influential living philosopher." Born in Australia, he is best known for his book* Animal Liberation, *which helped to spark the modern animal-rights movement. He was a cofounder of the International Association of Bioethics and founding coeditor of the journal* Bioethics. *Currently, he serves as professor of bioethics at Princeton University and laureate professor at the University of Melbourne. In his book* One World: The Ethics of Globalization, *Singer argues for the necessity of global rather than national ethical systems. Here, he discusses his notion of a global ethic in light of the war in Iraq, focusing on the United Nations and the International Criminal Court. He also tells us that "we bear responsibility for the inequalities of the world while we enjoy our luxuries"—and what to do about that.*

Question: You have discussed a world with one atmosphere, one economy, one law, and one community. Is it possible to bring all of these "ones" into one state, say, the United States of Earth? A state with no trade barriers, where the environment is everyone's concern, where all people share the same human rights and democratic representation? Is this something we should work towards? And if so, how?

Peter Singer: Really you are asking whether a kind of world federalism is a desirable and feasible goal, as something we should work towards. I would say it is a desirable goal, but we ought not to be seduced by the goal into thinking that we can bring that about in any short-term future. That would be a delusion and would probably mean forgoing more concrete, more specific things we can do to make the world better, which will not directly bring about that goal but might be stepping stones towards it. In other words, the idea of a United States of the Earth is really, at this stage, somewhat utopian. But it is a goal toward which we can take first steps, like trying to strengthen existing international organizations.

In *One World,* I talk about trying to strengthen the United Nations and what kind of reforms of the United Nations we might want to see. I have to say that some of those reforms seem further away now than they were when I wrote *One World.* I had not expected that a member of the United Nations would act in flagrant defiance of what a majority of the Security Council appears to think, as the United States is about to do in going to war in Iraq. That makes it in one way more difficult in the short-term. But perhaps in the medium-term, there will be a wider discussion of how to change the UN and how to make it more effective. That is one thing that we do need.

Other changes needed include having global environmental policies. Obviously, the Kyoto Protocol is a step towards that. We ought to be working to get the United States to conform to either Kyoto or to some revised agreement that will be no less effective —and hopefully more effective—in reducing global warming. As far as the WTO is concerned, I have also suggested ways of allowing environmental and social concerns to play a role.

So, I think we can work for these specific changes. And we should, in the immediate future, be focused on the specific changes rather than the larger and more distant goal. What is important is that the specific changes are in no sense inconsistent with that larger goal.

Question: Aristotle wrote that any type of world government would be tyrannous because even if the leader knew what was right, there would be others in the world who, knowing their own cultural values, even if they were wrong, would be convinced that they were right. Thus to enforce whatever is right, the leader of the world would be necessarily tyrannous. How would you respond to that? Is a world government, a *just* world government, really possible?

PS: I think that the response to that question has to draw a distinction between procedures and content of the decisions that come out of those procedures. The argument that you just suggested against a world government is equally an argument against a national government in any country where there is diversity of cultures and views, as there is in this country. You never expect unanimous consent in the population of the United States for any decision that Congress or the president makes. You never expect unanimous agreement with the substance of what is being decided, whatever that issue is, whether going to war with Iraq or using embryos for stem cell research. But you expect respect for the democratic decision procedure. If you think that the procedure that led to the election of the body that reaches these conclusions was carried out fairly, you can say you will respect that law and obey it, even though you disagree with it, because you want to show your support for the democratic decision procedure. I don't see why that can't happen in a world in which we have instant global communication. I don't see why that can't happen on a global scale just as well as it can happen on a national scale.

Question: In *One World,* you wrote about the necessity of global ethics and justice and mentioned the creation of the International Criminal Court. Despite the opposition of the Bush administration, this court finally opened officially in March 2003. How active a role do you anticipate the court to play in international justice, and how effective will it be given that it does not have the support of the U.S. government?

PS: The International Criminal Court exists to try to produce a global law against genocide and crimes against humanity. I believe that it can function effectively without the United States. Clearly, it would function more effectively with the United States. But a substantial number of countries have signed on— the last count that I saw was eighty-three—and therefore have agreed, essentially, to submit their nationals to the International Criminal Court if they are charged with crimes against humanity or crimes of genocide.

What we are going to get is a court that has cases to try and that does try them and that will gradually build up a body of experience and jurisprudence in dealing with such cases. I hope that eventually it convinces a future administration of the United States that it is dealing with these cases in a proper manner, that is not a kind of a political kangaroo court out to get any particular country but a serious judicial body that is trying to make sure there are global standards for some of the most serious crimes that can be committed, and that there is no place to hide from those kinds of crimes.

Question: In the arguments for basic universal values, a number of people have spoken on the wonderful and essential richness that comes from interfaith dialogue. You seem to have a number of doubts about the likelihood of global agreement on ethical questions or what you call factual questions, such as the existence of God. Why do you believe this? By agreeing on factual questions, do you mean choosing atheism?

PS: First, I think there are some common elements of many ethical systems. Those ethical systems that have been most fully developed are in civilizations that have a long written tradition of discussing ethical questions. The common elements seem to me to be things like saying, "To act ethically, you must put yourself in the position of your neighbor." Or indeed, not just your neighbor, which perhaps is something that comes from a smaller-scale society than we have now, but all the people around the world who might be affected by your actions. I think you can find that idea as basic in Christianity, Judaism, Islam, Confucianism, and Hinduism, as well as secularist and humanist traditions. You can find some agreement in a kind of universal ethics. But this is at a very broad and abstract level, not the level of particular principles, which say, for example, you should not clone human beings, you should not destroy embryos, brain death is to be regarded as death, or when exactly a war is just. Those are more specific things that we find it hard to get agreement on. I am not at all disparaging efforts to reach greater consensus.

But let's move to the second part of your question—whether people take their ethical view from a particular belief in God or in the divine status of a particular body of scripture. There is the idea that a particular body of scripture was divinely inspired or reflects the word of God. Then we have different bodies of scripture that tell us different things, quite apart from the fact that they can be interpreted in different ways even if we are working with the same body of scripture, which makes it much harder to get anywhere. You can see that by the fact that Christians, just to take one example, are obviously deeply divided on a whole range of issues. President Bush says that he is a Christian. Clearly, his view on the legitimacy of the war in Iraq is very different from many Christians, including the pope and many Protestant Christian leaders, too. You do not even get agreement within the one group.

In terms of the factual question about the belief in God, I was reflecting on historical experience that it seems extremely difficult to get agreement between people on their views of whether there is a divinity or not. If someone takes an ethical stance that is committed to a particular belief in God, or to a belief in a particular set of scriptures, then you cannot really expect to get agreement with other people with very different views. Does that mean that atheism is what you ought to be starting from? Well, I think it means that if you are really trying to reach agreement or present ethical views in ways that can reach everyone—reach us by virtue of the fact that we share a common ability to reason and understand—you are going to have to put in parentheses your views about God and a particular scripture. It does not mean you should drop them, but it means that you should realize that they are particular to you and they are not a sound basis for reaching agreement with other people who have different views about whether there is or is not a God and whether a particular body of scripture is or is not divinely inspired.

Question: As a utilitarian philosopher, you believe that human beings are morally obligated, or at least morally impelled, to give up that portion of their income not necessary for a comfortable existence to charitable causes for the betterment of the world's population. It cannot be ignored that having a child is very expensive. Is it immoral, therefore, to have three children when you could only have two and therefore save lives in the Third World? Can you put a number on the number of children one couple can morally have?

PS: I think that, indeed, having children or engaging in other serious commitments are morally significant questions because we need to think about the fact that what we spend is money that we cannot use to help people in the Third World or to help causes that we think will improve the world. Is having children specifically, therefore, wrong? There is one factor that does worry me in the long run about the idea that we should urge people not to have children in order to use the money to help good causes. From the evolutionary point of view, if you suggest to people not to have children in order to put their efforts into good causes generally, and if that message is not universally followed—as of course it won't be—it will be followed by those who are more responsive to ethical messages. If there is something genetic that makes people open to altruistic behavior or to messages about ethics (and this is only a hypothesis), then there is a real danger that you will eliminate it from the population, in which case the world will be even a worse mess than it is today. So that is why that would not be my first recommendation as to the expenditures that you ought to forgo in order to be able to do more for the Third World.

Question: How do you handle your salary as a teacher, and what thoughts do you have for college graduates who may, through work in law firms or investment banks, or sometimes through inheritance, be dealing with thousands or hundreds of thousands of dollars?

PS: As many of you will know, I have suggested that essentially anything we spend on ourselves for purposes of luxury is money that we are not spending to help people who lack the most minimal health care, who are not able to send their children to a couple of years of primary school, who are not really even able to see that their families get enough to eat. We bear responsibility for the inequalities of the world while we enjoy our luxuries. Many people say, "Well, what do you do about that?"

I am happy to be open about that. I do not do everything that I should be doing. I think my life still has too much indulgence in it. But I do give about 20 percent of what I earn to organizations like Oxfam America and other organizations that I think are making a difference to reducing the suffering of the world's poorest people. I do not see that as a static figure. I have gradually increased the amount that I have given over the years, and I will continue to do so. It is partly the standards that are around you that make you not want to give up too much of what you see everyone else is enjoying around you. So the environment you are in makes a difference.

I think you can all start working on that. You will find, as I did, that giving quite significant sums of money is actually not something that detracts from your own lifestyle in a way that is terribly harmful or a real sacrifice in the personal sense. It actually creates a level of satisfaction and fulfillment in the idea that you are living your life in a conscious, purposeful way that is contributing to making the world a better place. That many times makes up for whatever it might be that you are giving up.

Now people do talk to me about their careers. Should I go and work for an NGO that will pay me $30,000 a year, or should I go down to Wall Street and work in investment banking, where I will get three times as much—and in a few years will get a lot more still? I think there are reasonable things to be said on both sides, if you are really committed. The person thinking about going into investment banking may say, "Look, once I am earning $100,000, it will be a lot easier for me to give $10,000 or $20,000 or $30,000 away than if I am only earning $30,000. Obviously, I would need most of that to survive." On the other hand, if you work for the NGO, your talents and abilities are going to that organization directly.

Although I see the case for the other side, I tend to favor the NGO career. I tend to favor it because I worry about people whose values may change because of the environment in which they live. Now you are surrounded at school with a lot of people who think like you—perhaps many of whom might be part of this course. You cannot really see that there is great significance in whether you get to drive a BMW or whether you get to have your own yacht or your own house in the Hamptons or wherever else it might be. But who knows, give yourself five years in investment banking, and where are your values going to be after that, given the people with whom you are likely to be working? Some of you may be able to maintain them, but it will take a strong character to do so. If you are really convinced that you can stay committed, it would be great to have people with strong senses of values in those fields.

6. *DISTANCE AND PROXIMITY*
Closing the Gap

PAUL FARMER, physician

Paul Farmer is a globe-hopping medical doctor whose life's mission is to share the advances of modern medicine with those who need it most. While in medical school, he helped establish the community-based health organization the Clinique Bon Sauveur in Cange, Haiti, the poorest country in the Western Hemisphere. He is also one of the founders of Partners In Health, which works with local communities in the less developed parts of the world to deliver comprehensive health care and fight for social justice. The subject of the best-selling book Mountains Beyond Mountains *by Tracy Kidder, Farmer divides his time between Haiti and Harvard, where he is a professor of medical anthropology and an attending physician at Brigham and Women's Hospital. In this conversation, Farmer, a noted writer, speaker, and activist, discusses the inequalities of the world and the obligation to combat the dual epidemics of poverty and disease.*

Question: Upon hearing about the poor and the Third World, many people would like to help but do not. What specifically moved you to go to Haiti, immerse yourself, and help them?

Paul Farmer: That is a good way to start. I was born in Massachusetts, but I grew up mostly in Florida. I was your typical high school student, and although I was around migrant farm workers a little bit, it wasn't in any sensible or meaningful way. Nowadays I meet high school students who tell me, "I am already involved in a clinic for migrant farm workers, or writing letters to this organization, or working as a volunteer for that organization," and I think, "Oh, my God, I did not do anything useful like that when I was in high school."

But after I got to college, I was deeply interested and deeply involved. As a college senior, I got involved in migrant farm worker issues through a group called the Friends of United Farm Workers. I got interested in Haiti well before I ever got there, and it was because of Haitian migrant farm workers living here in this country. Some of them were living in such bad conditions that I was forced to ask, "Why would they leave their home country to be treated so badly here?" (Just to give you an idea of how bad is bad, when I was a college student, there were actually slavery charges brought against growers in the United States who were mistreating their migrant farm workers.) I wanted to be able to respond to a challenge a migrant farm worker had posed to me, "If you want to know why I left Haiti, you should go there and find out for yourself." So, between college and medical school, I went to Haiti.

I also thought I wanted to be a doctor. People say, so-and-so in my family is a doctor or so-and-so in my family was sick, neither of which happened in my case. I don't know why I wanted to be a doctor, but I did. I thought that I would learn Spanish and Haitian and practice in an American city, maybe Brooklyn. This is what I was trying to figure out during my first year of medical school. But what I saw in central Haiti was so compelling that I never left. In fact, the hospital of which I am medical director, along with one of my Haitian colleagues, is in the same squatter settlement that I first visited during the summer of 1983. I have been living between Harvard and Haiti ever since.

So, an answer to your question is involvement with migrant farm workers; understanding the connection between my country of origin and Haiti and then, later, other countries; and understanding that these are stories of proximity and not distance.

We are connected to Haiti in important ways, as well as to other places where there is violence and poverty and suffering. Proximity and understanding how the forces of poverty and injustice affect people's lives are things I wish you could get from reading books or seeing films. Sometimes you can if people are really good at conveying complexity in writing or on film. For me, engagement with the issues themselves made a big difference.

Question: In your fight against the almost overwhelming crisis of HIV/AIDS and the global inequities in health care, do you ever reach a point when you decide you have done a good job or done enough, even if you haven't reached your utopian destination? If you never do reach that point when you feel you have made enough progress, how do you keep momentum and energy and idealism alive?

PF: You said "almost overwhelming"; I would just go ahead and say "overwhelming." Who said I am not overwhelmed? I find it completely overwhelming. People constantly ask us, "How are you keeping the work going in Haiti?" especially now, just a few days after the overthrow of democratically elected president Jean-Bertrand Aristide. Our work has not stopped, and it will not stop, because we work with Haitians living in their home villages as well as with Haitian health professionals. The work *cannot* stop. In other words, I am working with a community of people and not solo, by any stretch of the imagination. When one of us feels overwhelmed, there are others on the team who might not feel overwhelmed. My colleagues and I remind each other, "If they, the people we are serving and who are living with these awful conditions"—and I am not talking only about diseases but also about having to worry about feeding your kids or getting clean water—"if they do not despair, then how can we arrogate despair for ourselves?" How can we say we are going to allow ourselves to be despairing or hopeless? This just may be an effective strategy for keeping sane: be connected to others who are not overwhelmed at the same time that you are, and realize that the people you serve are not allowing themselves to feel overwhelmed and despairing. Those are two important parts of the answer to your question.

A third antidote to despair, for me, would be the things I like about being a clinician, whether as a doctor, nurse, social worker, or another person providing direct services. In our work, even when you are losing the battle on the grand scale, you can still have small victories with individual patients or their families. In my line of work, which is infectious diseases, most people do get better. For a person in rural Haiti living in horrible poverty and with AIDS—if you treat her correctly by getting her on the medications she needs and providing her with the necessary social support—she will actually get better, even though the conditions around her might not improve anytime soon. We all want big victories that we can point to as adding up to something, as changing the world. Everybody wants that. But even when you cannot convince yourself that your work is meaningful on that scale, there are still small victories.

Now, that might sound a little bit craven, as though I am saying, "Well, if the definition of success is too daunting, just ratchet down the definition of success." I am not saying that; I am saying it is important to be mindful of the need for large victories and to not feel overwhelmed, but it is also important to be mindful of the fact that the small victories are important, too. Sometimes they are all you are going to get.

Question: In your interview with Caleb Hellerman, you stated that the average cost of HIV treatment in the U.S. would be in the range of $10,000 per patient annually compared to the $1,500 annually for those treated by your organization in Haiti. How have you been able to work with drug companies? Have you succeeded in obtaining price cuts despite the fact that it hurts their high profitability and their bottom line?

PF: I have some updates for you from the time that interview was conducted, and most of the news is good. First, however, I should point out that the $10,000 I cited, the lowball U.S. estimate, is probably the cost of the medications alone. I do not think that estimate includes lab work, physician and nurse costs, and certainly not hospitalization. As for the second figure, it now costs around $150 per patient per year for a good three-drug combination—reduced dramatically from $1,440, which was a concession price from the research-based pharmaceutical industry.

To answer the first part of your question, How have we done it? We did it through coalition building. We did it by working with the World Health Organization (WHO), Doctors Without Borders, and a group called the International Dispensary Association; there are also other players now on the scene, such as the Clinton Foundation. One person whose work you should follow is Jim Kim, who was the director of Partners In Health for some time, and who is now at the WHO. He has been very involved in negotiating and building up systems for drug procurement that have helped drop the price of drugs for tuberculosis and HIV and will continue to do so.

The second part of the question is the really hard part. The research-based pharmaceutical companies can reasonably argue, I suppose, that they have to be profitable, or their stockholders will not be satisfied. I am not an investor, but I can understand their point of view. However, I would say in honesty that the profitability of the drug companies is not my concern. My concern is for the welfare of my patients. I am not saying that to irritate. I think there is a mutual respect between doctors and people involved in the research-based pharmaceutical industry, so it does not seem unreasonable for someone who is a physician to not concern him- or herself with the profitability of pharmaceuticals but rather with the welfare of the patients at hand.

That said, let me review my response. One, we have continued to drop the price of antiretroviral therapy, to around $150 per patient per year. Two, coalition building is how we did it. Three, the profitability issue is not my primary concern. The question of funding is a real dilemma, and I do not know the answer. We have to find a way to finance drug development for the diseases of the poor. There must be a way, perhaps through a mix of public and private resources. After all, the everyday cash flows of the international financial markets are unthinkably huge. There are also enormous cash flows in the public sector and in the international financial institutions such as the World Bank and the International Monetary Fund. Those are not private cash flows; those organizations are publicly funded by member states and, ultimately, by citizens.

Furthermore, I think most of you know already that the research-based pharmaceutical industry is the most profitable of all international commerce, year in and year out. It has the highest return on investments, and it spends more on advertising than it does on research and development. Where do I get this information? From left-wing conspiracy magazines like *Fortune*. You get this information right from their own literature!

Those facts are important to have in the debate. But we also have to acknowledge that research-based pharmaceutical companies are under great pressure to produce high returns for their investors. We are not going to alter this structure of the modern corporation in time to develop new meds for diseases that afflict the poor. We have to create novel funding strategies.

Question: It seems that you have chosen to balance your life more in favor of the good works you do than your family or other things that might bring you more personal happiness. Do you ever regret the little time that your chosen path leaves for friends and family?

PF: Most of my friends and family are all involved in the same work I do. If I told you what my daughter said to me yesterday about the current situation in Haiti, you would never believe it. She said that she wanted to go to a demonstration. Now, if she says something like this to people who are not deeply involved in this line of work, they are going to think we are brainwashing the kid —she is only six. But she did say it. I did not tell her to say it. It is true; you cannot make this stuff up. It is really a different issue for me; the natural affiliation of my own friends and family and associates is really around the work we all do.

Everybody needs escape to life's simple pleasures—laughter and forgetting and so on. But sometimes laughter and forgetting come at a pretty high price psychically because the world is so riven by the problems that you are considering in this class. The striking thing about the world, to me, is its inequalities. Fifty years after the development of effective treatment, tuberculosis was still the leading infectious killer of adults in the world until it was surpassed by HIV disease. That is crazy. People die of diseases for which there are vaccines that cost twelve cents.

The question of making meaning in difficult times—everybody grapples with that. I am certainly not satisfied or self-satisfied. I keep asking myself, "Am I doing enough? Are we doing enough?" But rarely do I ask, "Is this meaningful at all?" For me, what I do is the most compelling thing I could be doing.

Question: You had said that as members of the community, we must recognize that we can and should summon our collective resources to save the countless lives that were previously alleged to be beyond our help. How can the average citizen go about summoning the resources to further your cause?

PF: First of all, I think we should regard the condition of our lives, of modernity in the twenty-first century, as different. Consider medicine: no one, certainly no one in infectious disease, would confuse the early twenty-first century with the mid-twentieth century. No one would deny that only sixty years ago the practice of modern medicine was completely different from and far inferior, in most ways, to what it is now.

A few days ago, I was talking to a professor at Columbia about Haiti and what is going on there now. He said, "It ought to be harder to do this in 2004 than in 1965 or 1953." I think I knew what he was talking about; historical events in Africa and Guatemala would be my guess as to what he was referring to. He spoke of political violence, and that the conditions of modernity ought to make things different not only in medicine but in terms of unnecessary suffering in general.

That is the first step: to acknowledge that the twenty-first century is a whole new ball game. People argue about globalization, about when it started. Did it start in 1492 or really in 1980? But modernity is different. We have the tools. Look at the information revolution or the revolution in medicine in terms of diagnostics and therapeutics. I go between a really fantastic hospital, the Brigham and Women's Hospital here in Boston, and rural Haiti. If you are on that Harvard–Haiti axis, you cannot help but think, "My God, what we could do with the fruits of science and modernity in a place like rural Haiti."

We have tried to do just that: move resources down the slope of inequality. Some lessons come from Haiti to us, but the tools and the fruits of modernity are largely controlled by us, people living in affluence. When I invoke the affluent, I do not just mean people in our country or Europe or Australia or Japan or an affluent Haitian living in Miami. I mean wealthy people everywhere in the world. By "wealthy," I do not mean Bill Gates–style wealthy; I mean all of us with access to resources like education, computers, modern medicine.

Those are my two points. One: modernity is different. Two: the fruits of modernity are unevenly shared. That leads me to answer the question in a very specific way. We should acknowledge our privilege and acknowledge the fact that the fruits of modernity are not shared equitably, and then ask strategic questions. How can we share them? How can students share them? The list is pretty much infinite. You can work on drug development, or raise money for Africans living with HIV, or coordinate policy forums or film screenings relevant to the questions that you ask. You could make a contribution to the remediation of inequalities and unnecessary human suffering in any one of a dozen, two dozen, or three dozen ways.

For me, as a teacher of medical students, as a doctor, and as an anthropologist, I think that it is probably not a good idea for me to be prescriptive and say, "You should do it this way rather than that way." In my experience, one of the things that people need to do is to figure out what appeals to them personally. If you are going to devote time to good works when you already have plenty of other things to do, then you have to like what you are doing. It has to be appealing to you because of another condition of modernity: the impression that there is not enough time. I feel that terribly, the time pinch. When I get involved in things that I consider to be compelling causes, it has to be something that I do not dislike doing, and I hope that is not too Arcadian. For example, I could not be a full-time policy maker working in a think tank. I just would not be good at it. I have to be around patients. But other people love that sort of thing and are good at it, and we need those people. Maybe the last thing that you expected me to say is, "It depends on your personality," but I really would link that to the first point, that modernity is different. The hard part is figuring out what you like to do and how you can remain engaged over time.

When I meet with medical students and encourage them to be involved in student activism, which I do all the time, in the back of my mind I am thinking that these people are soon going to be interns, and then they are going to be working eighty hours a week. Now, how are you going to tack on something else when you are already working eighty hours a week? You have to love it. I hope that does not sound like a touchy-feely Oprah-style answer, with all due respect to Oprah, because I mean it in a very practical way. Find out what you like to do and then do it. The condition of modernity is all about inequality and connection, and those things anybody can discover. But the real trick, I think, is finding your own best way to contribute.

AMY GOODMAN, *journalist*

Amy Goodman believes that it is the role of reporters "to go to where the silence is and say something." Passionate, thorough, and uncompromising, Goodman has done just that. The host and executive producer of Democracy Now! —*the largest U.S. public media collaboration and the only national radio and TV news show completely free of corporate underwriting—Goodman presents a range of voices often unheard in mainstream media. She has won numerous awards for her radio documentaries "Drilling and Killing: Chevron and Nigeria's Oil Dictatorship" and "Massacre: The Story of East Timor," including the Robert F. Kennedy Prize for International Reporting and the Alfred I. DuPont–Columbia Award. Her recent book,* The Exception to the Rulers, *coauthored with her brother David, examines how media monopolies and other corporate influences are undermining democracy. In this interview, Goodman recounts her personal stories from the field—from interviewing President Clinton to marching alongside Timorese as they protested years of Indonesian occupation and genocide.*

Question: Many students are eager to make a difference in the world by doing some kind of work that serves others. However, while there are lots of jobs in banking and consulting, there seem to be few jobs in sectors where serving others is possible. When you graduated from college, did you feel like it was risky to go to New York and volunteer for a radio station when your classmates were joining investment banks? What did your life look like?

Amy Goodman: First of all, I had taken five years off during college. I had left Harvard because I was so busy protesting outside that

I felt I was not exactly taking advantage of the courses. At that time, my activism was focused on the anti-apartheid movement and Harvard's huge investment in apartheid South Africa. But I did come back to Harvard with a keen interest in nutrition and the politics of food and nutrition. I pursued a degree in anthropology and did my thesis on a contraceptive drug called Depo-Provera, which is injected into a woman every three months. At the time, Depo-Provera was not approved by the FDA, and many people all over the world did not understand that it caused cancer in beagles and monkeys. In this country, I learned that ten thousand black women in Atlanta, Georgia, had been injected with the shot not knowing that it was not approved by the government. I could not afford to go overseas for my thesis to investigate how it was being injected into women in Thailand and other places, so I went down to Atlanta, Georgia.

When I finished the thesis, I had to defend it. In doing all this research, I thought, "What a difference it makes for women to understand the effect of drugs and particularly how they affect women." During my defense, I sat before the panel of professors in anthropology. One of them looked at it as he smoked his pipe. He asked, "Miss Goodman, do you understand what anthropology is? Because this is not an anthropology thesis."

I said, "Why is that?"

He responded, smoking on his pipe, "Because anthropology, Miss Goodman, is looking at someone else's culture, being an outsider looking in. You seem to have missed somewhere in your education the basic principles of anthropology."

So I said, "Well, using that definition, I am looking here at white, male, corporate science in the United States. It is not a culture I am part of, so I think it really does fit the definition of *anthropology.*"

Puffing on his pipe, he said, "Carry on."

Finishing and defending the thesis, I thought this was not going to particularly help this professor. I did not expect that *he* would be injected with Depo-Provera. But it would matter to a lot of people. We take for granted the level of research that people do in college classes that could help so many people. I finished school and went back home to New York to turn the thesis into a series of articles with a classmate named Krystyna von Henneberg. The articles came out in an issue of the *Multinational Monitor* called "The Case against Depo-Provera." (By the way, Depo-Provera has since been approved by the FDA and is being used by women, maybe even some of you, here in this country.)

One day while working on the articles at home at my parents' house, I turned on the radio, and I heard this amazing radio station, WBAI. I did not grow up with it, even though I grew up in New York. I thought, "What is this I am listening to?" It was so authentic, so real. I could hear all of the accents of New York City, none of which were trying to sell you anything. All of the glory and horror of New York was right there. I was transfixed. I thought it was a wonder how you could get involved with something like this.

I saw that there was a class in radio documentary being offered at Hunter College, where I was taking a graduate class in biochemistry in light of my interest in biochemistry and nutrition. I thought, "That is the class; that is radio documentary like that radio station I listen to." So I went over and joined the first class. It turned out that the teacher was a producer at WBAI, and

he was starting a program the next week called "Investiguy-
tions." (He had a speech impediment: he was from Australia.)
He said I could apprentice with him. We walked over to WBAI
that night, and I never left.

I found at the beginning of my career what people, if they are
lucky, find at the end of their career, and that is independence. I
volunteered for a time working with him. Be persistent in all of
your activities, whatever you do; if you want to volunteer, volunteer hard, volunteer a lot of hours. If you get a low-paying job to
do something at the beginning, just work a lot. Your hard work
absolutely pays off. He got a grant to investigate the Hiroshima
bombing forty years later, and he was able to pay me a little bit.
Then I quickly joined the newsroom doing pieces and then went
on staff. That investment at the beginning made an enormous
difference. I did the news for ten years and then did the morning show.

In 1996 we started *Democracy Now!* which was the only daily
election show in public broadcasting. Now it is nine years later,
and this radio program that broadcast in a couple dozen radio
stations a few years ago is now the largest public media collaboration in the country. We broadcast in over 350 Pacifica radio
stations and affiliates, NPR stations, and public access TV stations. (By the way, public access TV is a wonderful place to make
your own media.) We are now broadcasting on PBS stations, and
we broadcast on Dish Network, channel 9415, which is Free
Speech TV, and on Link TV, which is on DISH Network channel
9410 and DirecTV channel 375. We also video and audio stream
on the Web at democracynow.org and across radio stations
throughout Canada, Australia, and Europe. Two to three stations are picking us up a week. The whole idea is doing unem-

bedded, independent, international, grassroots news reporting. That is where I got my start.

Question: When describing your interview with former president Bill Clinton, Michael Powell of the *Washington Post* said that you are the reporter who sinks her teeth in and never lets go and that your questions prompted Clinton to scold, "You have asked questions in a hostile, combative, and even disrespectful tone." Is it necessary or worthwhile to ask the difficult questions in a tone like Clinton describes? Are the difficult questions more or less effective when they are asked this way?

AG: First of all, I think it is important to point out that that is how Clinton characterized it, because those in power interpret any kind of questioning in that way. We describe in detail what happened that day in *The Exception to the Rulers.*

It was Election Day 2000. Remember that day that we thought would end with learning the results of who would be president of the United States but we found out five weeks later who would be, no, not elected but selected? That morning, we were about to go on the air. It was about two minutes to nine. No one calls us at that time unless there is a breaking story because we have so much to do. We get a call: "Hi, this is White House Communications."

I thought they said "White Horse Communications," which is a tavern in New York where Dylan Thomas died by drinking himself to death. I could not understand why they would be calling, so I said, "What do you want?"

They said, "The president would like to talk to you."

I thought, "The president of the White Horse Tavern? And he's awake at nine o'clock in the morning?"

So I said, "The president of what?"

"The president of the United States."

"Oh." Now it is one minute to nine, and they are screaming for me to get into master control and I heard the music go on. So I said, "Whatever. Yeah, he can call. We will pick up the phone."

I did not really believe it, but I did not want to put this on the producers who were getting ready for the show. So I just said, "Guys, I think they said the president of the United States might call, so think of some questions as we are doing the show." He did not call for the hour.

Once we were done, we were going to have coffee. It was going to be a long day, since it was Election Day. We were just about to leave when the Latin music programmer screams from master control, "The president is on the phone!" We race in. The programmer was almost paralyzed. He had all of the music faders up and all of the microphones down. And you hear in the salsa music, "Hello, is anyone there?" It was the president of the United States. I jump over the control board. I push up all the faders for the microphones so the whole room is hot. Every microphone is on. Then I bring down the music, and I say, "Yes, Mr. President. Um. I understand you are calling to get out the vote. Why should people vote? Many people feel that both the Republican and Democratic Parties are captured by the corporations. What difference does a person's vote make?" He answered the question. And he was still there.

I then asked, "What about Leonard Peltier, the Native American leader?" Leonard Peltier had been convicted of killing two FBI agents in the mid-1970s. Due to alleged FBI and prosecutorial misconduct, many believe that Peltier had an unfair trial. President Clinton was considering whether to grant him clemency. It would be the first time he would address that issue. Mind you, I had not planned for this. But he was on the phone, and no one had ever asked him about this publicly, and he talked about it, saying he would make a decision. (Clinton ultimately did not grant clemency to Peltier, who still remains imprisoned in Leavenworth Federal Penitentiary. Clinton did, however, grant clemency to Marc Rich, a billionaire fugitive ex-husband of Clinton donor Christine Rich, and to several people associated with Clinton's half-brother, Roger Clinton.)

Then I asked him about the death penalty and why he chose to go back in his first term, when he was running for president, to preside over the execution of Ricky Ray Rector, who was brain damaged. I then asked him about the racial disparities and all the studies that had come out about who gets the death penalty. President Clinton said this was why we should vote for Hillary Clinton and Al Gore. I was a little confused. I said, "Well, why? They are for the death penalty." And he said, "Well, yes, but they understand those studies." I was thinking, "Well, wait a second, so it is better to vote for someone who is for this and understands the implications than someone who does not understand the implications and is for this?" Then I asked him about the sanctions against Iraq at the time and about the UN secretary and assistant secretary generals, too, who had quit saying they were genocidal. He said they were liars. I asked him about Ralph Nader. I asked him about racial profiling. Al Gore said if he were president, as the first act in office he would outlaw it. But I said, "You were both in power for eight years. Why did you not do it then?" It was the promise versus the record.

At some point, Clinton made that comment about my tone. I had given him a chance, in full, to answer every question. But I think the reason he said that was because presidents rarely get

asked tough questions. In this country, journalists treat them as
royalty on bended knee. Presidents are simply the employees of
the American people. When this opportunity arose, I felt it was
my responsibility to ask the questions so many people had asked
for so long. For example, people are curious about the napalming and bombing of Vieques, this island that was part of the
United States. Vieques, which is part of Puerto Rico, was appro-
priated by the U.S. Navy as a bombing target; this led to pollu-
tion, the ruining of the livelihood of thousands, and ultimately
the murder of a Vieques resident.

The next day, the White House called and basically said
I would be banned from going to the White House. I said,
"What are you talking about? He called me. I did not call him."
They said that I did not follow the protocol. And I said, "What
protocol?"

"The questions we'd agreed to."

"Who'd agreed to?"

They said, "We said that he would talk about getting out the
vote. Maybe questions one, four, and seven of your questions
were related, but the others . . ."

I said, "I had made no agreement. I submitted no questions
to you."

They said, "We said he had two or three minutes."

I said, "For God's sake, he is the most powerful man in the
world. He can hang up if he wants to!"

We talk about this incident in *The Exception to the Rulers,*
what it means and why it is that these kinds of questions are not
asked. It makes me think of Elisabeth Bumiller of the *New York
Times,* who recently was asked at a forum why they did not ask
tougher questions on the eve of the invasion with one of President Bush's extremely rare news conferences. She said—I am

paraphrasing—because the weight of history was on our shoulders. That is exactly when you ask the question, when you look at how many U.S. servicemen and -women have died in Iraq. If those questions are not asked, it does a disservice to the servicemen and -women of this country, not to mention how many Iraqi civilians have died. Tens of thousands of people the U.S. administration supposedly went in to liberate and to save are now dead. I did not consider it hostile questioning. I simply considered it doing my job.

Question: You have dedicated your life to a career in pursuit of journalistic integrity. In retrospect, do you think it is necessary to forsake the idea of family given your own experiences as a successful reporter, journalist, and activist? Do you have any regrets or feel as though you have missed out on something because you have dedicated your life to social activism?

AG: I don't know who actually said this, but it was a quote that always sticks with me: "I think back on my life at all the times I thought I went too far. I realize now I did not go far enough." There is just so much that has to be done. It is not about sacrifice, though. I get great joy out of my work. Family can be defined in so many different ways; I have a wonderful family that I was born into, and the people I cover, in many cases, have become extended family. It is incredible the entrée that you have into people's lives with just a microphone and the trust that they place in you.

I will briefly tell the story of East Timor, which is a story that we write about in *The Exception to the Rulers*. The idea is what all media should be and has fallen far short of; the media has reached an all-time low in this country. But it is not just about media. I think the most important role to play in life is as the exception to the rulers.

How many of you know the story of East Timor? I bet you

know it for one of two reasons: possibly Noam Chomsky, who wrote about it forever, or because of independent media. You are not going to get it from other places in this country. Corporate media hardly covered this for well over a decade. It is one of the worst genocides of the twentieth century. Indonesia invaded East Timor in 1975, just as East Timor, a small Catholic country that had been colonized by Portugal for many years, was gaining their independence from Portugal. Henry Kissinger was secretary of state. Gerald Ford was the president. They went to Indonesia and met with Suharto, the long-reigning Indonesian dictator, the day before the invasion and gave the go-ahead for the invasion. On December 7th, 1975, the Indonesian military invaded East Timor by land, by air, by sea, killing thousands of Timorese, then tens of thousands. They closed the country to the outside world, and for the next seventeen years, they killed off a third of the population, proportionately worse than what happened in Cambodia.

In 1990 I got a chance to go to Timor with my colleague Allan Nairn. We found a true hell on earth. In 1991 we went back because for the first time a delegation commissioned by the UN was going to investigate the human rights situation. We wanted to see what happened. Allan and I followed a procession one day, November 12th, 1991, of a thousand people that walked from the main Catholic Church in Dili, Timor, three hundred miles north of Australia. On this day, the people were marching from the church to the cemetery. Many of the people were college age. There were thousands marching. Old women in the traditional Timorese garb. Girls in their Catholic-school uniforms. Boys in their school shorts. They marched and they unfurled banners that they had written on bed sheets that said things like, "Why did the Indonesian military shoot our church?" They appealed to President Bush senior, they appealed to the UN, they appealed to anyone to do something about this killing field.

In a land of no freedom of assembly, no freedom of press, no freedom of speech, the Timorese's march to the cemetery was the biggest act of civil disobedience the Indonesian military had ever seen. When they got to the cemetery at about eight o'clock in the morning, everyone was crowded around. They were exhilarated, though very afraid. Thousands more had joined from home, work, and school. Then we saw from the direction the procession had come hundreds of Indonesian soldiers carrying their U.S. M-16s at the ready position. People at the back were hemmed in by the walls of the cemetery. The soldiers marched up, twelve to fifteen abreast. Allan and I were asking people, "Why are you here?" They would say, "For my mother. For my sister. For my brother. For my village that was wiped out." Then we saw these soldiers marching up. I put my headphones on. I always hid everything so that the soldiers would not see us interviewing Timorese. It would only endanger them. But now we knew the only hope might be if the soldiers saw Western journalists. They had committed many massacres in the past, but never in front of Western journalists. I put my headphones on and held up my microphone like a flag. Allan put the camera above his head. At the time, he was writing for *The New Yorker* magazine; I was doing a documentary for Pacifica Radio. We walked to the front of the crowd. The soldiers marched up, still twelve to fifteen abreast. They rounded the corner. Without any warning, without any hesitation, without any provocation, they swept past us and opened fire on the crowd, gunning people down from right to left. The first to go down, a little boy behind us, exploded from the gunfire. And they kept on shooting.

The soldiers beat me to the ground. Allan got a photograph

of them opening fire, and then he threw himself on top of me to protect me from further injury. They took their U.S. M-16s, and they slammed them against his skull until they fractured it. We were lying in the road, covered in blood. Timorese were being killed all around us. A group of the soldiers came up and put their guns to our heads in firing squad fashion. They were screaming "Politik! Politik!" because to bear witness is political. They were also screaming "Australia!" Were we from Australia?

We knew what had happened to the Australian journalists in 1975 at the time of the invasion. They had lined five of them up against a house and executed them. There was one left. The day after the invasion, they dragged the last man, Roger East, who was reporting for *The World* out of the radio station in Dili, the capital. As he shouted that he was from Australia, they shot him into the harbor. The Australian government hardly raised a peep about these killings, maybe because a few years later they would sign the Timor Gap Treaty with Indonesia, dividing up the oil spoils that belonged to Timor between Indonesia and Australia. Oil has been the source of so much pain in the world.

As we lay on the ground, we said, "No, we are not from Australia. America. America." We were stripped of everything at that point, still lying in the road. The only thing I had left was my passport, and I threw it at them. At some point, they decided to take the guns from our heads. We believe because we were from the same country their weapons were from, they would have to pay a price for killing us that they had never had to pay for the Timorese. They moved on.

A Red Cross Jeep pulled up, and we got into it. Dozens of Timorese jumped on top of it and on top of us. We drove like that, as a human mass, to the hospital. When we got to the hospital, the doctors and nurses started to cry when they saw us. We were not in worse shape than the Timorese. Hundreds of Timorese were killed on that day—more than 270—and that number matters. But I think they cried because of the things we represent to the people not only of East Timor but all over the world: one is the sword and the other the shield. We are the sword because all too often the U.S. government provides military weapons to repressive regimes or uses them against other populations themselves. But Americans also represent the shield. It is the idea that every little act we engage in makes such a difference in the world because we come from the most powerful country on earth. Just a call to a Congress member or a walk to Harvard Square in protest for workers' rights is heard around the world. Especially when you come from the most powerful institution in the most powerful country in the world, it makes an enormous difference. They know that. On that day, that shield was bloody; it just increased their despair.

By 1999, the people of East Timor finally got a chance to vote. Incredible what they had asked for all those years. And in 2002, they won their freedom. Allan Nairn and I returned on May 19th, 2002, to join with the people of East Timor to cover them as they celebrated their independence. Out on the sandy plain of Tasi Tolo, outside of Dili, the people gathered a hundred thousand strong. As the clock struck midnight, Xanana Gusmão, the rebel leader of East Timor, now the founding president, ascended the stage and raised the flag of the Democratic Republic of East Timor. The people looked up at the fireworks display, and you could see the light of the display in their tear-stained faces. This nation of survivors had won. They had resisted, and they had won, though they had paid an unbelievably high price.

They won because of their own persistence and resistance, but also because of the solidarity of people all over the world. They knew they could not do it without them. It left an indelible image, and it follows me everywhere I go, every day I do the broadcast.

Whatever age you are, whatever you are doing—whether you are a student or a professor, employed or unemployed, a janitor, a painter, working in the school bookstore or the cafeteria— every hour of every day we have a decision to make. And that is whether to be the sword or the shield.

SOURCES

Introduction

WORKERS AS ANONYMOUS BENEFACTORS: *Nickel and Dimed,* by Barbara Ehrenreich (2001).

HARVARD LIVING WAGE CAMPAIGN: The history of the campaign, the historic student sit-in at the president's offices, and the ongoing efforts to eradicate poverty wages at Harvard can be found at www.hcs.harvard.edu/~pslm/livingwage. Greg Halpern's *Harvard Works Because We Do* (2003) is a collection of interviews and photographs of Harvard workers taken at the time of the campaign.

Howard Zinn

CHANGING ATTITUDES AND BELIEFS: *You Can't Be Neutral on a Moving Train: A Personal History of Our Times,* by Howard Zinn (2002).

THE AMERICAN DREAM: "Growing Up Class Conscious," excerpted from Zinn's *You Can't Be Neutral on a Moving Train: A Personal History of Our Times* (2002).

PREEMPTIVE WAR: "The Case against the War in Iraq," by Howard Zinn, *Boston Globe,* August 19, 2002.

THE ATOMIC BOMB: *Hiroshima,* by John Hersey (1989).

UNITED STATES HISTORY: *A People's History of the United States: 1492–Present,* by Howard Zinn (2003).

FACTORY WORKERS UNIONIZE: See information at Jobs with Justice at www.jwj.org/WRBs/success/BostonRichmark.htm.

RELATED READINGS AND RESOURCES

Black Boy, by Richard Wright (1945)

Born on the Fourth of July, by Ron Kovic (1976)

Howard Zinn: You Can't Be Neutral on a Moving Train, 78-minute documentary film directed by Deb Ellis and Denis Mueller (2004)

Johnny Got His Gun, by Dalton Trumbo (1939)

Living My Life, by Emma Goldman (1930)

The Zinn Reader: Writings on Disobedience and Democracy, by Howard Zinn (1997)

Elaine Scarry

IMAGINING OTHERS: Scarry's essay "The Difficulty of Imagining Other Persons" appears in *The Handbook of Interethnic Coexistence,* edited by Eugene Weiner (1998).

LITERATURE IN ETHICAL AND POLITICAL DISCUSSIONS: See, for

example, *The Fragility of Goodness: Luck and Ethics in Greek Tragedy and Philosophy* (2001) and *Poetic Justice: The Literary Imagination and Public Life* (1997), both by Martha Nussbaum; and *Contingency, Irony, and Solidarity,* by Richard Rorty (1989).

BEAUTY AND JUSTICE: *On Beauty and Being Just,* by Elaine Scarry (1999), *The Fate of the Earth,* by Jonathan Schell (2000), and *Silent Spring,* by Rachel Carson (2002).

NONSYMMETRICAL THINKING: "A Nuclear Double Standard," by Elaine Scarry, *Boston Globe,* November 3, 2002. See www.commondreams.org/views02/1103-01.htm.

DETERRENCE THEORY: "The Growing Nuclear Peril," by Jonathan Schell, *The Nation,* June 6, 2002.

COMMAND AND CONTROL OF NUCLEAR WEAPONS: *Fire in the East: The Rise of Asian Military Power and the Second Nuclear Age,* by Paul Bracken (2000).

OPERATION TIPS (TERRORISM INFORMATION AND PREVENTION SYSTEM): See www.commondreams.org/headlines02/0716-01.htm.

RELATED READINGS AND RESOURCES
  The Body in Pain: The Making and Unmaking of the World, by Elaine Scarry (1987)
  "Citizenship in Emergency: Can Democracy Protect Us against Terrorism?" by Elaine Scarry, *Boston Review* 27, no. 5 (October/November 2002). See www.bostonreview.net/BR27.5/scarry.html.
  Dreaming by the Book, by Elaine Scarry (2001)

Noam Chomsky

CHOMSKY'S CHILDHOOD: "Conscience of a Nation," by Maya Jaggi, *Guardian,* January 20, 2001.

PROGRAM ON INTERNATIONAL POLICY ATTITUDES: See www.pipa.org.

RELATED READINGS AND RESOURCES
  9-11, by Noam Chomsky (2001)
  Hegemony or Survival: America's Quest for Global Dominance, by Noam Chomsky (2003)
  Manufacturing Consent: The Political Economy of the Mass Media, by Noam Chomsky and Edward S. Herman (1988)
  "The Loneliness of Noam Chomsky," by Arundhati Roy, *The Hindu,* August 24, 2003. See www.thehindu.com/thehindu/mag/2003/08/24/stories/2003082400020100.htm.

Robert Reich

INTERNATIONAL LABOR STANDARDS: The International Labour Organization's labor standards serve as the benchmark by which the rights and conditions of human beings at work are measured. See www.ilo.org/public/english/standards/norm/.

SWEATSHOPS: "American Sweatshops," by Robert Reich, American Prospect Online (www.prospect.org), January, 18, 2001.

MILITARY SPENDING: "Take a Guess: Who's Going to Pay for the Terror Economy?" by Robert Reich, American Prospect Online (www.prospect .org), October 23, 2001.

RELATED READINGS AND RESOURCES
  Reason: Why Liberals Will Win the Battle for America, by Robert Reich (2004)
  See Robert Reich's Web site at www.robertreich.org/reich/books.asp.

Juliet Schor

AMERICANS AND CONSUMPTION: *The Overspent American: Why We Want What We Don't Need,* by Juliet Schor (1998).

COMMERCIALIZATION OF CHILDHOOD: Schor's book about the commercialization of childhood is called *Born to Buy: The Commercialized Child and the New Consumer Culture* (2004).

CONSTANT TELEVISION HOUSEHOLDS: Refer to the Kaiser Family Foundation's report "Kids and Media at the Millennium" (1999).

LEISURE TIME: David Barsamian interviews Schor in "The Overworked American: The Unexpected Decline of Leisure," *Z Magazine,* January 20, 1993. See http://zena.secureforum.com/Znet/zmag/articles/barschor.htm.

RELATED READINGS AND RESOURCES
  The High Price of Materialism, by Tim Kasser (1999)
  Sustainable Planet: Solutions for the 21st Century, by Juliet Schor and Betsy Taylor (2002)
  Adbusters (www.adbusters.org)
  Center for a New American Dream (www.newdream.org)
  Commercial Alert (www.commercialalert.org)
  Worldwatch Institute (www.worldwatch.org)

Aaron Feuerstein

RESPONSIBILITY TO WORKERS: "They Call Their Boss a Hero," a profile of Aaron Feuerstein by Michael Ryan, *Parade,* September 8, 1996.

MILITARY PRODUCTS: Malden Mills manufactures a range of products for military use, including the quick-drying, flame-resistant Shipboard

Blanket and the water- and windproof Foul Weather Parka. Information and photographs of these and other military products can be found at www .polartec.com.

LAWRENCE, MASSACHUSETTS: Built in the 1840s, Lawrence, Massachusetts, is located twenty-five miles north of Boston, along the Merrimack River. It is the nation's first planned industrial city and home to Malden Mills.

Naomi Klein

HALLIBURTON: "Bring Halliburton Home," by Naomi Klein, *The Nation* (www.thenation.com), November 6, 2003.

FENCES AND WINDOWS: With money from the royalties of her book *Fences and Windows: Dispatches from the Front Lines of the Globalization Debate,* Klein founded the Fences and Windows Fund to raise money for grassroots groups organizing and educating on themes related to neoliberalism and war. Additional information about the fund as well as the preface to Klein's book can be found at www.fencesfund.org.

RELATED READINGS AND RESOURCES
   No Logo: Taking Aim at the Brand Bullies, by Naomi Klein (2000). See www.nologo.org.

Lani Guinier

INTERSECTIONALITY: "Intersectionality, Identity Politics, and Violence against Women of Color," by Kimberly Crenshaw, *Stanford Law Review* 43, no. 6 (1991).

WOMEN IMPRISONED BY MEN'S DREAMS: *Prisoners of Men's Dreams: Striking Out for a New Feminine Future,* by Suzanne Gordon (1991).

AFFIRMATIVE ACTION AND HIGHER EDUCATION: The two lawsuits that challenged University of Michigan admissions policies were decided by the U.S. Supreme Court in June 2003. Background information and court filings can be found at www.umich.edu/~urel/admissions/.

SWEATT V. PAINTER: In 1946 Heman Marion Sweatt, an African American, applied for admission to the University of Texas Law School, a then-segregated institution, but was rejected. With the support of the NAACP, Sweatt sued, and his case went to the United States Supreme Court, which ruled in support of integration in 1950. The archives of that historic case can be found at www.law.du.edu/russell/lh/sweatt/.

VOLVO EFFECT: Peter Sacks explores the "Volvo effect," a term he coined in his book *Standardized Minds: The High Price of America's Testing Culture and What We Can Do to Change It* (2000).

LSAT EFFECTIVENESS: *Becoming Gentlemen: Women, Law School, and*

Institutional Change, by Lani Guinier, Michelle Fine, and Jane Balin (1997).

TEN-PERCENT PLAN: The Civil Rights Project at Harvard University published "Percent Plans in College Admissions: A Comparative Analysis of Three States' Experiences," by Catherine L. Horn and Stella M. Flores (2003). See www.civilrightsproject.harvard.edu/research/affirmativeaction/tristate.php.

PROPORTIONAL REPRESENTATION: *The Tyranny of the Majority: Fundamental Fairness in Representative Democracy,* by Lani Guinier (1995).

RELATED READINGS AND RESOURCES

    The Miner's Canary: Enlisting Race, Resisting Power, Transforming Democracy, by Lani Guinier and Gerald Torres (2003)

Katha Pollitt

WOMEN, CHILDREN, AND CAREERS: "Backlash Babies," by Katha Pollitt, *The Nation* (www.thenation.com), May 13, 2002.

ABORTION: "In the Waiting Room," by Katha Pollitt, *The Nation* (www.thenation.com), April 21, 2003.

RELATED READINGS AND RESOURCES

    Reasonable Creatures: Essays on Women and Feminism, by Katha Pollitt (1995)

    Subject to Debate: Sense and Dissents on Women, Politics, and Culture, by Katha Pollitt (2001)

Martha Minow

FORGIVENESS: *Breaking the Cycles of Hatred: Memory, Law, and Repair,* edited by Martha Minow and Nancy L. Rosenblum (2003)

TRUTH AND RECONCILIATION COMMISSION: Information about the documentary film *Long Night's Journey into Day* (2000), directed by Frances Reid and Deborah Hoffman, can be found at www.irisfilms.org/longnight/.

RELATED READINGS AND RESOURCES

    After Jihad: America and the Struggle for Islamic Democracy, by Noah Feldman (2003)

    Between Vengeance and Forgiveness: Facing History after Genocide and Mass Violence, by Martha Minow (1999)

    "A Problem from Hell": America and the Age of Genocide, by Samantha Power (2003)

    What We Owe Iraq: War and the Ethics of Nation Building, by Noah Feldman (2004)

    Facing History and Ourselves, www.facinghistory.org

Swanee Hunt

BOSNIA: In her book *This Was Not Our War: Bosnian Women Reclaiming the Peace* (2004), Swanee Hunt presents interviews with twenty-six women who survived the Bosnian war.

GENDER FAIRNESS: "Inclusive Security: Women Waging Peace," by Swanee Hunt, *Foreign Policy*, July 2004.

NANDA POK: Founder and executive director of Women for Prosperity, Nanda Pok publishes a magazine promoting women in leadership and trains women for political office. An article about her work appears at www.womenwagingpeace.net/content/articles/0386a.html.

RWANDAN WOMEN IN LEADERSHIP: "Rwandan Women Step Forward," by Swanee Hunt, Scripps Howard News Service, October 8, 2003. The article appears at www.womenwagingpeace.net/content/articles/0305a .html.

RELATED READINGS AND RESOURCES
Women Waging Peace (www.womenwagingpeace.net)

Jennifer Leaning

PUBLIC HEALTH AND TERRORISM: "Public Health, War and Terrorism," by Jennifer Leaning, *Harvard Health Policy Review* 4, no. 1 (Spring 2003). See www.hhpr.org/currentissue/spring2003/leaning.php.

PRISONS IN AFGHANISTAN: "A Report on Conditions at Shebarghan Prison, Northern Afghanistan," Physicians for Human Rights (January 2003). See www.phrusa.org/research/afghanistan/report.html.

RELATED READINGS AND RESOURCES
International Committee of the Red Cross (www.icrc.org)
Physicians for Human Rights (www.phrusa.org)

Harvey Cox

DIANA ECK AND RELIGIOUS PLURALISM: Diana Eck is the author of *A New Religious America: How a "Christian Country" Has Become the World's Most Religiously Diverse Nation* (2002). She is also the director of the Pluralism Project, whose mission is to help Americans engage in the realities of religious diversity (www.pluralism.org).

THE MARKET GOD: "The Market as God," by Harvey Cox, *The Atlantic Monthly*, March 1999.

KARL POLANYI: Polanyi's seminal book *The Great Transformation* (1944) critiques the philosophical and historical foundations of economic liberalism.

SALE OF HUMAN ORGANS: "Thinking the World—Gould, Dershowitz, and Cox Cross Swords and Ideas in Class," by Andrea Shen, *Harvard*

Gazette, April 13, 2000. See www.news.harvard.edu/gazette/2000/04.13/think.html.

RELATED READINGS AND RESOURCES

The Secular City: Secularization and Urbanization in Theological Perspective, by Harvey Cox (1965)

When Jesus Came to Harvard: Making Moral Choices Today, by Harvey Cox (2004)

Peter Singer

ONE WORLD: *One World: The Ethics of Globalization,* by Peter Singer (2002).

KYOTO PROTOCOL: The Kyoto Protocol (1997) is an international agreement to reduce the greenhouse gas emissions causing climate change. The Bush administration withdrew support for the Kyoto Protocol in March 2001. The full text of the Kyoto Protocol can be found at http://unfccc.int/resource/docs/convkp/kpeng.html.

ARISTOTLE: In *The Politics,* Aristotle discusses different types of governments as well as the potential for tyranny.

RELATED READINGS AND RESOURCES

The President of Good and Evil: The Ethics of George W. Bush, by Peter Singer (2004)

International Criminal Court (www.icc-cpi.int)

Oxfam America (www.oxfamamerica.org)

Paul Farmer

SLAVERY OF MIGRANT FARM WORKERS: The Coalition of Immokalee Workers' Anti-Slavery Campaign has worked with the Civil Rights Division of the Department of Justice to investigate and prosecute modern-day slavery cases. More information about specific cases can be found at www.ciw-online.org/slavery.html.

HIV TREATMENT COSTS: "Interview with Paul Farmer," by Caleb Hellerman, www.inequality.org/haitidoctor.html.

RELATED READINGS AND RESOURCES

AIDS and Accusation: Haiti and the Geography of Blame, by Paul Farmer (1992)

Infections and Inequalities: The Modern Plagues, by Paul Farmer (1999)

Pathologies of Power: Health, Human Rights, and the New War on the Poor, by Paul Farmer (2003)

The Uses of Haiti, by Paul Farmer (1994)

Women, Poverty, and AIDS: Sex, Drugs, and Structural Violence, edited by Paul Farmer, Margaret Connors, and Janie Simmons (1996)

Partners In Health (www.pih.org)

Amy Goodman

DEPO-PROVERA: "The Case against Depo-Provera," by Amy Goodman, *Multinational Monitor,* February/March 1985.

CLINTON INTERVIEW: "The Annotated Interview with President Clinton: The People Respond," November 7, 2000. See www.democracynow.org.

LEONARD PELTIER: *In the Spirit of Crazy Horse, by Peter Matthiessen (1992); Prison Writings: My Life Is My Sun Dance, by Leonard Peltier,* edited by Harvey Arden (2000). Also see the Leonard Peltier Defense Committee Web site, http://leonardpeltier.org.

NAPALMING AND BOMBING OF VIEQUES: *Islands of Resistance: Puerto Rico, Vieques, and U.S. Policy,* by Mario Murillo (2001).

STATE OF THE MEDIA: Comments of Elisabeth Bumiller of the *New York Times* are included in Amy Goodman's interview with veteran White House correspondent Helen Thomas (April 8, 2004). See www.democracynow .org.

CONFLICT IN EAST TIMOR: Noam Chomsky has written extensively on this subject, including the article "Why Americans Should Care about East Timor," *Mother Jones,* August 26, 1999. See www.chomsky.info/articles/ 19990826.htm. Also refer to *Funu: The Unfinished Saga of East Timor,* by José Ramos-Horta (1986), *A Dirty Little War,* by John Martinkus (2001), and the Web site of the East Timor Action Network, http://etan.org.

RELATED READINGS AND RESOURCES

The Exception to the Rulers: Exposing Oily Politicians, War Profiteers, and the Media That Love Them, by Amy and David Goodman (2004)

Democracy Now! Web site, www.democracynow.org

ACKNOWLEDGMENTS

This is a book *about* human community, but it is also a *product* of such a community. We wish to thank the sixteen dedicated individuals who agreed to be interviewed for the class and the book, receiving no compensation except our deep gratitude. Also deserving thanks are the Harvard students who worked into the wee hours preparing questions and the teaching fellows who guided them along the way. Then there are those who have sustained the four of us editors in the journey from course to book. We cannot name them all here, nor embarrass them sufficiently with public expression of our affection, but we want especially to acknowledge Kim Adams, Samuel Brown, Carole Bundy, Moa Forstorp, Allan Hunter, Kit Jaeger, the Palmer family, Joel Pulliam, Saydi Shumway, and Christopher Vyce. Thanks also to the Stockholm Institute of Education.

INDEX

abortion, 150–152, 159
activism: anti-apartheid, 244;
    definitions of, 112–113; in Haiti,
    47; and media, 58, 112–113, 118,
    251–256; in 1960s, 46; personal
    accounts of, 107–108; 233–236;
    student activism, vii–ix, 107–110,
    145–146, 233–234, 240–242, 255.
    See also civil rights movement;
    political protest
Adams, John Quincy, 44
advertising: and children, 87, 210–
    211, 213; and consumption, 81;
    and pharmaceuticals, 238; and
    politics, 70; as propaganda, 52–
    55; and religion, 214; in the sky,
    217. *See also* media
affirmative action, 126–129, 137,
    141
Afghanistan, 11, 153, 194, 197–198,
    201
African Americans: in the armed
    forces, 128; civil rights, 5, 10, 38;
    and feminism, 153; and higher
    education, 123–124, 131–132,
    136–137, 142; women, 244.
    See also affirmative action
AIDS: in Africa, 192–193; cost of
    medication for, 237–239; treat-
    ment of, 236. *See also* Haiti
American Dream, 8–9, 81
anarchism, 7
Animal Farm (Orwell), 58
animal rights, xi, 221
anthropology, 241, 244–245
anti-globalization movement,
    116–119
Aristide, Jean-Bertrand, 18, 47, 49,
    235. *See also* Haiti

Aristotle, 223
Auden, W. H., 28
Australia, 254
Austria, 176–177

Bailey, Thomas, 45
Bill of Rights, 4, 40–41
Bosnia, 164, 170, 176–177, 182
Bourdieu, Pierre, 155
Bracken, Paul, 35
*Branded: The Buying and Selling
    of Teenagers* (Quart), 210–211
Brazil, 218
Buddhism, 219–220
Bumiller, Elisabeth, 250
Bush, George H. W., 48, 253
Bush, George W., 9, 50, 74, 115, 148,
    225, 250; administration of, 15,
    19, 21, 33, 81, 89, 224

Cambodia, 180, 252
Canada, 50, 108, 114, 119–120
capitalism, 213, 217–219. *See also*
    economics; globalization; Market
    God
careers: and independence, 246;
    nonprofit versus Wall Street,
    228–229; and sacrifice, 251; and
    satisfaction, 133; of women, 91,
    146–149. *See also* personal
    choice; work
Carson, Rachel, 30
Carter, Jimmy, 48
Center for a New American Dream,
    81, 89–90
charity, 78, 226–228
children: advertising directed at,
    87, 210–211, 213; and AIDS,
    192–193; and consumer culture,

WBAI, 245–246; women's magazines, 156–158. *See also* advertising; propaganda
medicine (practice of), 233–242
Mexican Americans, 137. *See also*
Latinos
Mexican War, 14, 16
Mexico, 16, 50, 78, 117–118
migrant workers, 78, 114, 233–234
military (U.S.): and affirmative
action, 127–128; budget of, 7;
conduct of, 201–202; and history
of citizenship, 38–39; justification for intervention in foreign
countries, 16–19, 169–171; personal reflections on, 12–14, 21;
and subcontracts, 100–101
Milosevic, Slobodan, 170, 176
modernity, 204–205, 240–241
motherhood, 91, 146–148, 153, 155.
See also women

Nader, Ralph, 249
NAFTA, 66–67, 119
Nairn, Allan, 252–256
napalm, 12, 250. *See also* nuclear
warfare
national security (U.S.), 14, 32–34
Native Americans, 16, 44–45, 141,
248
neoconservatism, 150–151
neoliberalism, vii, 50–55, 117–118
Netherlands: labor laws in, 92
Nike, 109–110
9-11. *See* September 11
nongovernmental organizations
(NGOs), 116, 173–174, 228–
229
nonviolence, 40
Northern Alliance, 198. *See also*
Afghanistan
North Korea, 18, 34–35

nuclear warfare, 9, 31, 34–36.
See also Hiroshima
Nussbaum, Martha, 28

oil, 17, 49, 111, 180, 254
Orwell, George, 7, 58

pacifism, 17, 40
Paine, Thomas, 41
Partners In Health, 237
A Passage to India (Forster), 28, 30
Patriot Act, 33
peace negotiations, 175–178, 183–
184
Peltier, Leonard, 248
personal choice: in career and
family balance, 239–240; and
consciousness-raising, 143, 174;
and free will, 22; and learning
from failure, 184–186; and making meaning, 240; and NGO
versus investment banking, 228–
229; and perseverance, 186–187,
235–236; and responding to
poverty, 227–228, 234–235; and
sword versus shield, 256; and
using one's privilege, 204–206,
227–228, 241–242
pharmaceuticals, 244–245, 237–239
philanthropy, viii, 175
Philippines, 16, 118
philosophy: beauty and justice, 28–
30; thought experiments, 31–32,
171; utilitarianism, 226. *See also*
ethics; religion
Physicians for Human Rights, 203
Pok, Nanda, 180
Polanyi, Karl, 212
Polartec, 105
political correctness, 109
political protest. *See* civil
disobedience